# Earring Chic

## 35 Hand-Selected Projects

*Edited by Jennifer Claydon*

**NORTH LIGHT BOOKS**

Cincinnati, Ohio

CreateMixedMedia.com

# Table of Contents

JAPANESE DIAMONDS *by Rebeca Mojica*
*To learn how to make these earrings, see page 122.*

# A note from the editor . . .

Whether you're new to making jewelry or a seasoned hand at it, earrings make the perfect project for so many reasons! First, they're quick to make. If you want to add a special touch to an outfit, you can whip up a pair of matching earrings in just a few minutes. Or, if you're in need of a last-minute gift, you can quickly and easily create a lovely pair to present. Earrings are also great projects for those busy days when you don't have a lot of time to create, but still want a crafty fix. Even if you decide you want to create a fabulous, complex pair of earrings or use special techniques like chain mail, earrings take only a fraction of the time a necklace or bracelet would take using the same technique.

Not only are earrings great time-savers, they're economical when it comes to materials, too. You'll only need a small handful of supplies to create any of the projects in this book. Making your own earrings gives you fashion on a budget. On the other hand, if you decide to splurge on some special beads or precious metals, the short materials lists for these projects will keep the splurge small.

So dive into the pages of *Earring Chic* and find beautiful designs for all of your earring needs—there's a pair for every style and every skill level. The projects are divided by skill level, so start by exploring the projects that best suit your experience. Within each chapter we've gathered together a bevy of beautiful designs from talented designers including Heidi Boyd, Margot Potter, Sara Schwittek and more. In these pages you're sure to find a project that suits your style or a pair that lets you play outside of your style comfort zone. Have fun fashioning an entire new earring wardrobe for yourself!

BOMBAY HOOPS *by Sara Schwittek*
*To learn how to make these earrings, see page 64.*

# 1

# Getting Started

If you've made a piece of jewelry before, chances are that you already have on hand everything you'll need to make yourself a beautiful pair of earrings. If you're new to jewelry making, all the necessary supplies, materials and tools are just a short shopping trip away. You most likely have a local bead store or craft store nearby and that should be the first stop in your search. If you can't find what you need locally, well, a world of great jewelry supplies is at your fingertips on the Internet. Over the next few pages, you'll find descriptions of the most common items needed to stock your craft pantry for hours of happy earring making!

SNOW QUEEN *by Julie Ashford*
*To learn how to make these earrings, see page 96.*

# Beads and Findings

Doesn't your mouth water and your heart beat faster when you walk into a bead shop? So many delicious options—your mind begins to whirl with all the possibilities! Earrings are the perfect project not only for featuring those exquisite gemstone briolettes but also for using up all of those little odds and ends gathered in the bottom of your bead box. Here are just a few of the items you can use.

CRYSTAL BEADS Crystals are precision cut and bring beautiful sparkle to your earrings. They are available in countless colors, finishes, sizes and shapes, making them a staple in any bead stash.

GLASS BEADS Glass beads come in an endless variety of shapes, sizes and colors and can be an inexpensive alternative to pricier gemstones and crystal. They're generally very uniform in size and often have a larger hole size to accommodate thicker gauge wire or leather cording.

SEMIPRECIOUS STONES The natural organic beauty, texture and color in these treasures from the earth can set your pieces apart. They can range wildly in price and quality depending on their size, cut and clarity. Take into account their often irregular shapes and small holes when using gemstones in your designs.

WOOD AND NATURAL MATERIALS Wood, bone, shell and other natural materials can give your jewelry an earthy, organic quality. Most of these materials are inexpensive and will give your pieces a one-of-a-kind look.

PEARLS Freshwater pearls provide a timeless, classic feel to any earring design and are surprisingly affordable. Pearls come in a wide variety of shapes—rice, potato, coin and nugget to name a few—and are often dyed in beautiful shades.

HEADPINS Headpins are short pieces of wire with a flat head or a round ball at one end, often used to create dangles. Headpins come in different gauges, so test to see if they fit the beads you're using. Lengths from 1"–2" (3cm–5cm) will meet most needs.

CHAIN Chain is available in a wide variety of styles, sizes and finishes. Sterling silver and gold-filled chains will give your jewelry a more refined look, but gold-plated and silver-plated chains are a wonderful alternative when you need to stick to a budget. Chains also come in gunmetal, copper, brass and antiqued finishes.

SPACER BEADS Spacer beads may not be very exciting, but they're essential in beading. Spacers provide definition to your special beads or that extra attention to detail that adds visual value to your finished piece.

EARRING HOOKS There are so many beautiful earring hooks available at craft stores, bead shops and online, and using manufactured components can save a lot of time. However, be sure to see the techniques section for instructions on making your own unique hooks. It's easier than you think (pages 127 through 129)!

DECORATIVE COMPONENTS There are hundreds of chandeliers, connectors, charms and other decorative components available at craft and jewelry supply stores. Be creative when it comes to components—just because it's called a "clasp" doesn't mean you can't use it in an earring!

# Wire

When selecting wire for your projects, keep in mind the gauge and hardness of the wire. The higher the gauge number, the thinner the wire will be. All projects include gauge recommendations, but feel free to adjust the gauge to match the holes in your beads.

The hardness rating of the wire indicates how difficult it is to manipulate. Sterling silver and gold-filled wire are often available in dead-soft, half-hard and hard. Half-hard, round wire is generally a good choice.

Colored craft wire is inexpensive and comes in a rainbow of bright colors, but it can mar easily. You could be left with unattractive dents and scratches. Use coated wire in projects only when the color of the wire is more important than the durability of the finished piece.

## Wire Chart

When you buy sterling silver or gold-filled wire, it's often by the foot or by the troy ounce (31 grams). Use this handy chart so you know how much you're buying:

*20 gauge = 19' (6m) per troy ounce*
*21 gauge = 25' (8m) per troy ounce*
*22 gauge = 31' (9m) per troy ounce*
*24 gauge = 48' (15m) per troy ounce*
*26 gauge = 76' (23m) per troy ounce*
*28 gauge = 120' (37m) per troy ounce*

## Tip

*While you are learning, feel free to use less expensive silver-plated or gold-plated brass or copper wires. You can find them at most craft stores. Plated wire will generally not be designated as soft, half-hard or hard, so you can ignore these specifications in the project instructions, but do use wire of the recommended gauge.*

# Tools

The great thing about getting started with jewelry making is that you need only a few essential tools to make even the most beautiful designs. Most of these basic tools can be found at your local craft store, and none of the tools need batteries or electricity!

CHAIN-NOSE PLIERS The jaws on chain-nose pliers taper to a dull point. Use them to grip your wire while making wraps or bends. Make sure yours are smooth on the inside, because textured jaws will leave marks in your wire (top pliers shown).

SIDE OR FLUSH WIRE CUTTERS Use side cutters to cut wire to size, remove excess wire from loops and wraps, and trim headpins and chains. Flush cutters leave your ends a little tidier. Buy a pair with a small, clean point so you can get into tight areas (middle pliers shown).

ROUND-NOSE PLIERS Round-nose pliers have jaws that taper to a point. Use them to make wire loops. Round-nose pliers with very thin jaws make smaller loops, which makes jewelry look more delicate. Mark the spot that you like on the nose with a permanent marker so you can consistently make loops the same size (bottom pliers shown).

RULER Any ruler will work, but heavy-duty, stainless steel rulers with cork backings stay steady on work surfaces. Be sure the ruler includes both inches and millimeters, because many beads and findings are measured in millimeters.

NOTEBOOK, PENS AND COLORED PENCILS It's always a good idea to jot down the specifics of a design that you've just created so you can reproduce it easily again in the future. You never know when you'll be hit with a jolt of inspiration for a new design or color scheme. Record it with your colored pencils!

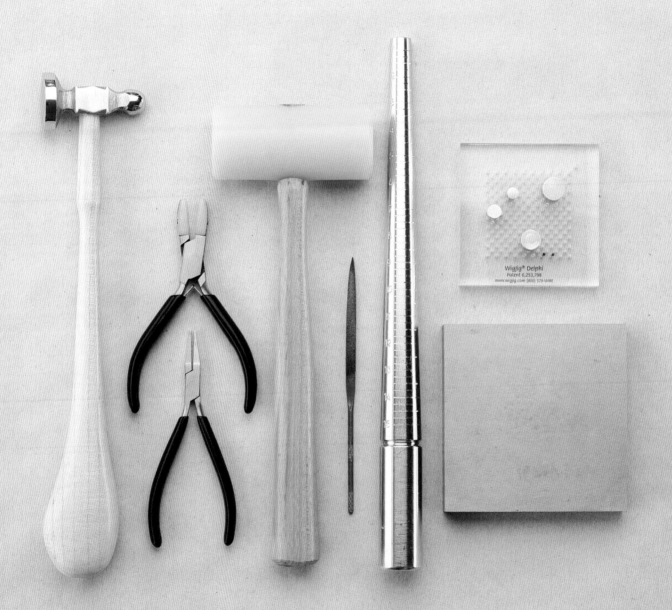

# Earring Hook Tool Kit

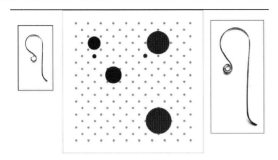

## Tip

*This diagram of a wire jig illustrates suggested layouts of various sized pegs to create two different sizes of earring hooks. See pages 127 through 129 to learn more about creating your own earring hooks.*

CHASING AND BALL-PEEN HAMMER This hammer typically has two heads: a slightly domed chasing end and a knobby ball-peen end. Use this hammer for adding textured, hammered effects in sterling silver, as well as for flattening wire and other metal components.

NYLON-JAW PLIERS These pliers have a plastic coating on the jaws that prevents marring on wire. Use them to straighten longer lengths of thicker wire or to work-harden the wire (top pliers shown).

FLAT-NOSE PLIERS These have a flat, squared-off tip. They have many uses, but you'll mainly use them to create wire spirals (bottom pliers shown).

HARD PLASTIC MALLET Use this tool to strike a metal object without marring or dinging it. Using this mallet ensures that the wire is not flattened. The striking action helps the metal retain its shape through the process of work-hardening (see page 135 for more information on work-hardening).

NEEDLE FILE Use this file to smooth sharp ends of cut wire, especially when creating earring hooks. You can use fine-grit sandpaper, a sanding stick, a sanding block or 0000 steel wool if you prefer.

RING MANDREL Typically used for sizing rings, you'll use this tool to create unique handmade hooks. You can also use wood dowels, smooth-barreled pens, markers or bottles to achieve the same effect.

WIRE JIG Use a wire jig when you need to make lots of earring hooks with a consistent shape and size. A jig set usually comes with a plastic or metal panel with a grid of holes and corresponding pegs of various diameters. Wrap your wire around these pegs to shape wire into endless forms; making earring hooks is just the beginning.

STEEL BLOCK Hammer on this flat, solid surface of hardened steel to prevent damaging your work surface. A mini anvil (not shown) is another solid surface option for hammering.

# 2

# Easy Earrings

If you're new to making jewelry, this chapter is the perfect place to start. Throughout the following pages you'll find easy earrings that will help you build your skills without sacrificing anything in the looks department. These easy projects are also quick and fun if you already have jewelry-making skills or if you want to dip your toe into a new skill. The *Easy Chain Earrings* on page 20 are a simple introduction to chain mail. If you want to improve your wire-wrapping skills, the *Sun and Sea Swing* earrings on page 46 give you plenty of practice.

Use the projects in this chapter to create earrings for every occasion. For an easy-breezy summertime feel, try the *Caribbean Collage* earrings on page 16. The *Wrapped Drop Stones* earrings on page 28 also have a pretty, casual feel, and they're easily altered to match the colors of your favorite outfit. If you're feeling artful, the *Twisted Leaf* earrings on page 26 may be a great match to your mood. For a more formal look in a flash, try the *Stone and Chain* earrings on page 44. Select truly spectacular beads for this pair, and they'll be simply stunning. And if it's sparkle you're looking for, the *Teal and Crystal* earrings on page 48 should suit your needs. Let these projects prove to you that simple doesn't have to equal plain!

WRAPPED DROP STONES *by Heidi Boyd*
*To learn how to make these earrings, see page 28.*

# Caribbean Collage

*By Sara Schwittek, from* Perfect Match

These earrings remind me of all the shells, stones and other little treasures I collected on the beach as a child. The mellow colors of the freshwater pearls and mother-of-pearl beads are intermixed with sparkling crystals that hint of the ocean. Use extra beads left over from other projects to create a medley of texture and color!

## MATERIALS & TOOLS

2—10mm–15mm silver circles

2—5mm × 8mm keishi (or cornflake) pearls

4—4mm white rice freshwater pearls

2—10mm recycled glass beads

2—10mm mother-of-pearl coin-shaped beads

2—6mm erinite Swarovski crystal bicone beads

2—4mm × 7mm pale aqua faceted rondelle beads

4—2mm × 3mm silver saucer spacer beads

4—4mm silver daisy spacer beads

1—4" (10cm) length of 26-gauge half-hard, sterling silver wire

12—2" (5cm) silver headpins

2—earring hooks

Wire cutters

Round-nose pliers

Chain-nose pliers

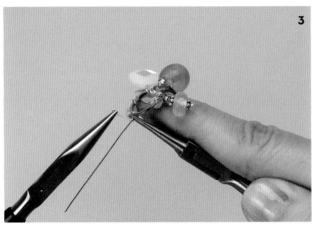

1 To create the bead dangles, slide each bead (except the keishi pearls) onto a headpin and create a simple loop on the top of each (see page 130 for instructions on creating a simple loop). Leave the loop open for now. To vary the visual texture, match some of the larger beads with accents like silver daisy spacers or smooth silver spacers.

2 Connect six of the bead dangles from Step 1 onto a silver circle and close the loops. Set this piece aside. Repeat for the other earring.

3 With 2" (5cm) of wire, begin to create an open loop and insert the silver circle with the dangles. Close the loop securely with two or three wraps.

4 On the tail of the wire, slide on one keishi pearl. Create a wire-wrapped loop at the top of the pearl and close it securely with two or three wraps (see page 131 for instructions on creating a wire-wrapped loop). Connect the earring hook into the top loop and repeat Steps 3 and 4 to make a second earring.

# Chain Link Tassels

*By Heidi Boyd, from* Simply Beaded Bliss

For a new twist on fiber tassels, hook multiple lightweight lengths of chain together on a handmade eyepin to make a lightweight metal tassel. The tassel is topped with an interesting mixture of wood, resin and shell beads. This design can be easily adapted by using chain with a different finish or by choosing chain made with smaller or larger links. If you change the chain, be sure to switch up the beads to match.

## MATERIALS & TOOLS

10—1½" (4cm) lengths of small link chain

2—blue resin beads

2—round wooden beads

2—small silver bead caps

2—small flower connectors

2—3" (8cm) lengths of 22-gauge silver-plated wire

2—earring hooks

4—small silver-plated jump rings

2—pairs of flat- or chain-nose pliers

Round-nose pliers

Wire cutters

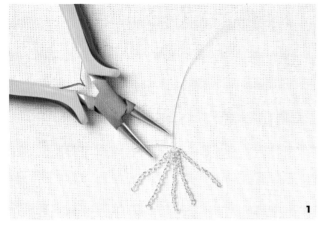

1 Use the center of the round-nose pliers to create a slightly larger-than-usual loop in one end of a piece of wire (see page 130 for instructions on creating a simple a loop). Hook the first link of each of five chain sections onto the wire loop. Wrap the loop closed (see page 131 for instructions on creating a wire-wrapped loop).

2 String the following sequence of beads onto the open wire end: blue resin bead, bead cap, wooden bead.

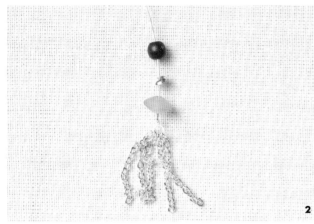

3 Shape the wire end into a regular-sized loop, and then wrap the wire around the base of the loop and trim the end. Link the tassel to a flower-shaped connector with a jump ring (see page 135 for instructions on opening and closing jump rings). Link the flower connector to an earring hook with a second jump ring. Repeat Steps 1 through 3 to make a second earring.

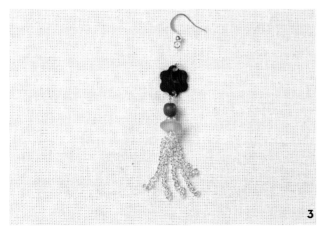

19

# Easy Chain Earrings

*By Rebeca Mojica, from Chained*

These earrings come together quickly, making them a perfect project for beginners. However, the color and sizing variations are endless, so more advanced students can feel free to experiment right off the bat. This pattern is a great one to have in your repertoire should you need to whip up a pair of earrings before you head out for a night on the town.

## MATERIALS & TOOLS

6—large jump rings: P16 anodized aluminum, color gold, 16 gauge, 5/16" (7.9mm)

8—small jump rings: F18 anodized aluminum, color purple, 18 gauge, 5/32" (4.0mm)

2—earring hooks

2—pairs of flat-nose pliers

## Tip

*If your earring hook loop is perpendicular to the hook instead of parallel to it, add a very small ring to the loop first, and attach your chain mail to that ring. Otherwise, your earring won't face forward.*

1 To prepare, close the small rings and open the large rings (see page 135 for instructions on opening and closing jump rings). Scoop two small rings onto an open large ring. Before closing, add an earring hook to the large ring.

2 With a new large ring, scoop up two new small rings, then weave the large ring through the two small rings from Step 1. It helps to pinch the previous small rings between your thumb and index finger for stability. Close the large ring.

3 With another large ring, go through the two small rings added in Step 2. Close the large ring, and you're done! Repeat Steps 1 through 3 to make a second earring.

*Try these earrings in your favorite colors, or make a pair to match a favorite outfit.*

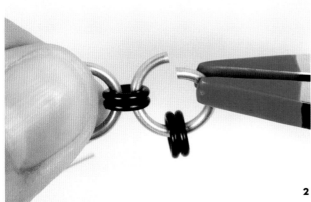

# Flower Bunch

*By Heidi Boyd, from* Simply Beautiful Beaded Jewelry

At first glance, the large faceted rose crystal beads in these earrings are what attract your attention. On closer inspection you'll discover the more subtle beauty of a delightful hanging bouquet of glass flowers and leaves.

## MATERIALS & TOOLS

2—10mm faceted pink beads
2—purple flower beads
2—small black flower beads
2—12mm × 18mm iridescent leaf beads
2—silver eyepins
6—1½" (4cm) silver headpins
2—lever back earring hooks
Round-nose pliers
Wire cutters

## *Tip*

*Change the appearance of the earrings by simply switching the bead color palette to green, black and white. If you're having trouble locating leaf and flower beads, substitute heart- and butterfly-shaped glass beads.*

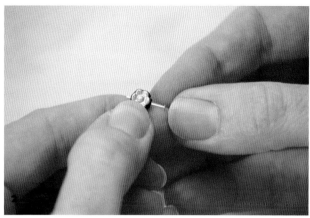

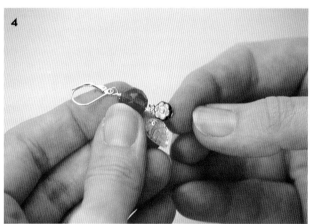

1 Thread a pink faceted bead onto an eyepin and make a loop at the top with the round-nose pliers (see page 130 for instructions on creating a simple loop). Slide the loop onto an earring hook and wrap the tail of the wire around the base of the loop (see page 134 for instructions on wrapping wire around a base). Trim off any excess wire tail with the wire cutters.

2 Slide a flower bead onto a headpin and trim the wire to about 3/8" (1cm) above the head. Make a small loop above the bead with the round-nose pliers. Repeat with another flower bead.

3 Slide a leaf bead onto a headpin and bend the headpin wire to a 90-degree angle. Create a loop in the top of the wire with the round-nose pliers so the headpin forms an S shape.

4 Attach all three of the dangles to the eyepin loop on the faceted bead by opening and closing the loops with the pliers. Repeat Steps 1 through 4 to make a second earring.

# Simple Elegance

*By Sara Schwittek, from* Perfect Match

These earrings are so fast and easy to make, you'll want them in every color! Be creative—changing the colors or materials transforms the entire mood of the earrings.

## MATERIALS & TOOLS

2—8mm pacific opal Swarovski crystal rondelle beads

2—4mm indicolite Swarovski crystal bicone beads

4—4mm silver daisy spacer beads

2—7mm fancy soldered-closed jump rings

2—2" (5cm) headpins

1–5" (13cm) length of 24- or 26-gauge half-hard sterling silver wire

2—earring hooks

Round-nose pliers

Chain-nose pliers

Wire cutters

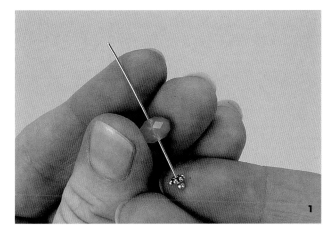

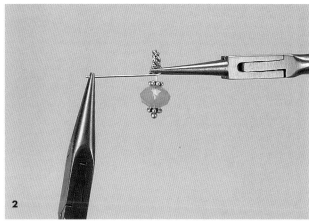

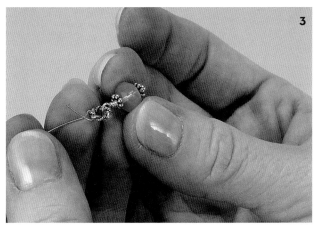

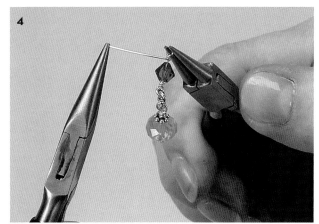

1 Start by sliding onto a headpin in order: one daisy spacer one 8mm crystal rondelle and one daisy spacer.

2 Begin to create an open loop. Insert the decorative jump ring into the loop and then close it securely with two or three wire wraps (see page 131 for instructions on creating a wire-wrapped loop). Put this piece aside.

3 With 2½" (6cm) of wire, create an open loop and add the jump ring with the connected rondelle. Close the loop with two or three wraps.

4 On the tail of the wire, slide on one 4mm crystal bicone. Create a wire-wrapped loop at the top of the bicone and close it securely with two or three wraps. Connect the earring hook into the top loop, and repeat Steps 1 through 4 to make a second earring.

# Twisted Leaf

*By Heidi Boyd, from* Simply Beautiful Beaded Jewelry

These tiny flowering stems are easy to create—just twist folded sterling wires together with your fingertips. Fresh-water pearl buds and miniature glass leaves are simply threaded onto the wires and then twisted into place. The length of the stems is completely adjustable. If you prefer, make smaller earrings with a single bud and one or two leaves, or extend the stem and add more pearls and leaves to make longer earrings.

## MATERIALS & TOOLS

2—blue-gray freshwater pearls

6—iridescent glass leaf beads

2—8" (20cm) lengths of 26-gauge sterling silver wire

1—pair sterling silver post earrings

Round-nose pliers

Wire cutters

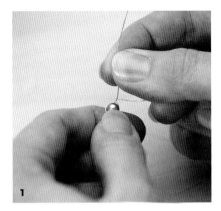
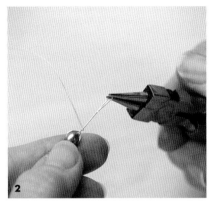

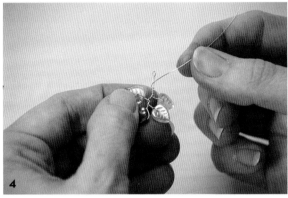
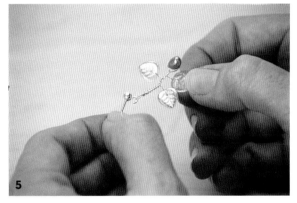

1 Cut about 8" (20cm) of wire and thread a freshwater pearl onto one end, about 2¹/₂" (6cm) or so from the end of the wire. Twist the wire together three times to secure the bead.

2 Measure up about ⁷/₈" (2cm) from the top of the twisted bead and then wrap one wire around the round-nose pliers to make a small loop that is open at the bottom with about ¹/₂" (13mm) of straight wire under the loop. This wire will form the center stem.

3 Thread a leaf bead onto the open wire, hold the leaf ³/₈" (1cm) away from the pearl, and fold the wire end back down toward the pearl. The leaf will be trapped on a wire loop.

Tightly twist the wire loop three times to create a short stem. Twist the wire three times around the central stem. Repeat to add two more leaves, separating each addition with three twists around the center stem wire.

4 Wrap the wire around the open end of the open loop shape to secure the opening.

5 Open the loop on the earring post and slide on the loop at the top of the twisted wire. Use pliers to close and secure the loop. Repeat Steps 1 through 5 to make a second earring.

# Wrapped Drop Stones

*By Heidi Boyd, from* Wired Beautiful

Wrapping the top of stone or pearl beads is a fabulous wire technique to master. The free-form wire wraps mirror the irregular shapes of the natural stone beads. As long as the wire can thread through the stone bead, the subtle differences are not important—they're what make the earrings uniquely handcrafted.

## MATERIALS & TOOLS

4—top-drilled colored stone beads

2—6mm sterling silver jump rings

20-gauge silver-colored wire

24-gauge silver-colored wire

2—silver-colored earring hooks

Round-nose pliers

Chain-nose pliers

2—pairs of flat- or chain-nose pliers

Wire cutters

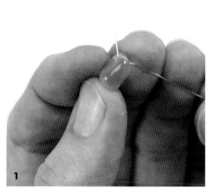

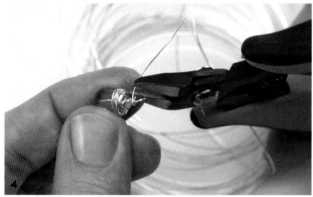

1 Working directly from the spool of 24-gauge wire, pass the wire through the top of the stone bead ½" (13mm). Bend the ½" (13mm) wire end up so it sticks straight out the top of the bead.

2 Wrap the other end of the wire around the round-nose pliers to form a loop.

3 Start wrapping the wire around the base of the loop, trapping the wire end in the wraps.

4 Continue wrapping the wire down around the top of the bead, concealing the wired hole. When you're pleased with

the wrapping, wrap twice more around the top of the wrap. Cut the wire off the spool with wire cutters. Tuck the end of the wire into the wire wrap. Repeat Steps 1 through 4 to wrap the three remaining stones. Form two earring hooks with the 20-gauge wire (see page 127 for instructions on creating simple earring hooks).

5 Link a jump ring to the hanging loop of one of the wrapped stones (see page 135 for instructions on opening and closing jump rings). Open the hanging loop of an earring hook; add the loaded jump ring and a second stone before closing the loop. Repeat Step 5 to make a second earring.

# Advertastic Chandeliers

*By Margot Potter, from The Impatient Beader Gets Inspired!*

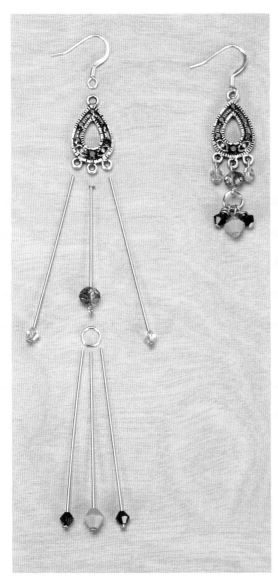

Vintage labels from the 1930s and 1940s were the inspiration for the colors in these crystal-and-metal chandelier earrings. I love the unexpected but delightful color combinations. Advertising art is an excellent source for striking color combinations, because it is created specifically to catch the eye.

## GMP PANCAKE EARRINGS

### MATERIALS & TOOLS

4—4mm jonquil AB Swarovski bicone beads

2—6mm crystal copper Swarovski round beads

2—6mm turquoise Swarovski bicone beads

4—4mm light Siam Swarovski bicone beads

2—light Siam crystal chandelier components

12—2" (5cm) 20-gauge headpins

2—4mm silver-plated jump rings

2—earring hooks

2—pairs of flat- or chain-nosed pliers

Chain-nose pliers

1  To make these earrings, put together the headpins as shown at left.

2  Attach a dangle with a simple loop (see page 130 for instructions on creating a simple loop) to each of the three loops in the chandelier component: jonquil, copper, jonquil.

3  Attach a jump ring to the copper round dangle and link three more dangles to the jump ring: light Siam, turquoise, light Siam (see page 135 for instructions on opening and closing jump rings). Wrap the headpin wire a few times around the tops of the beads.

4  To finish, add an earring hook to the top of each earring.

## *LITHIATED LIME EARRINGS*

### MATERIALS & TOOLS

4–6mm peridot AB Swarovski bicone beads

2–6mm jet Swarovski rondelle beads

2–4mm fire opal AB Swarovski bicone beads

2–4mm peridot AB Swarovski bicone beads

2–4mm jonquil AB Swarovski bicone beads

12–20-gauge silver-plated headpins

2–4mm silver-plated jump rings

2–jet crystal chandelier components

2–silver-plated earring hooks

2–pairs flat- or chain-nose pliers

Chain-nose pliers

1 Create the looped headpins with the 4mm bicone beads. Wrap the headpin wire a few times around the tops of the beads (see page 131 for instructions on creating a wire-wrapped loop).

2 Attach a dangle with a simple loop to each of the three loops in the chandelier component: peridot, jet, peridot (see page 130 for instructions on creating a simple loop).

3 Attach a jump ring to the jet rondelle and link three more dangles to the jump ring: fire opal, peridot, jonquil (see page 135 for instructions on opening and closing jump rings).

4 To finish, add an earring hook to the top of each earring.

## HAPPY DAY EARRINGS

### MATERIALS & TOOLS

2—9mm × 6mm tanzanite Swarovski teardrop beads

4—6mm hyacinth Swarovski bicone beads

4—5mm crystal AB Swarovski round beads

2—tanzanite crystal chandelier components

10—20-gauge silver-plated headpins

2—silver-plated earring hooks

Round- and chain-nose pliers

1 Create the looped dangles as shown by turning a loop in the headpin wire at the top of each bead (see page 130 for instructions on creating a simple loop).

2 Attach the dangles to the chandelier components using round- and chain-nose pliers in the following order: crystal round, hyacinth bicone, tanzanite teardrop, hyacinth bicone, crystal round.

3 Add the earring hooks to the top of each earring to finish.

## LITTLE MISS EARRINGS

### MATERIALS & TOOLS

2—6mm peridot AB Swarovski bicone beads

4—4mm jonquil Swarovski bicone beads

4—4mm indicolite AB Swarovski bicone beads

2—peridot crystal chandelier components

10—20-gauge silver-plated headpins

2—silver-plated earring hooks

Round- and chain-nose pliers

1 Create the looped dangles as shown by turning a loop in the headpin wire at the top of each bead (see page 130 for instructions on creating a simple loop).

2 Attach the dangles to the chandelier component using round- and chain-nose pliers in the following sequence: indicolite, jonquil, peridot, jonquil, indicolite.

3 Add the earring hooks to the top of each earring to finish.

# Aurora

*By Julie Ashford, from* Spellbinding Bead Jewelry

Long dangling earrings have a glamorous look that will put you in the mood for an evening out. These are made from strands of beaded headpins and eyepins cleverly joined together using a series of jump rings—it's really very simple!

## MATERIALS & TOOLS

8—4mm topaz AB crystal bicone beads

4—4mm pale jonquil AB crystal bicone beads

20—4mm pale pink AB crystal bicone beads

10—4mm rose pink AB crystal bicone beads

1 gram—galvanized apricot gold seed beads

1 gram—lined rose pink AB seed beads

1 gram—lined crystal/yellow luster seed beads

1 gram—pale yellow Ceylon seed beads

2—size 3 silver-lined crystal bugles

6—size 3 silver-lined gold bugles

10—size 3 silver-lined pink bugles

22—2" (5cm) gilt eyepins

10—2" (5cm) gilt headpins

10—³/₁₆" (5mm) gilt jump rings

2—earring hooks

2—pairs flat- or chain-nose pliers

Round-nose pliers

Wire cutters

1 Thread each of the ten headpins with the following: one pale pink bicone, one apricot gold seed bead, one pale pink bicone, one apricot gold seed bead, one lined crystal/yellow luster seed bead, one silver-lined pink bugle bead and one lined crystal/yellow luster seed bead. Trim the wire extending above the final bead to 1/4" (6mm) and make a loop (see page 130 for instructions on creating a simple loop).

2 Link each prepared headpin onto an eyepin. Onto each eyepin thread one apricot gold seed bead, one rose pink AB crystal bicone and one apricot gold seed bead. Trim the wire and form a loop, as in Step 1. Set two of these strands aside.

3 Attach an eyepin to each of the remaining eight strands. Onto the first two thread one lined rose pink seed bead, one topaz AB crystal bicone and one lined rose pink seed bead. Trim the wire and form a loop. Set these two strands aside. Onto each of the remaining six strands, thread on one lined rose pink seed bead, one topaz AB crystal, one lined rose pink seed bead, one silver-lined gold bugle and one lined rose pink seed bead. Set two of these strands aside.

4 Attach an eyepin onto the top of each of the four remaining strands. Onto each, thread one pale yellow Ceylon seed bead, one pale jonquil AB crystal bicone and one pale yellow Ceylon seed bead. Trim the wire and form a loop on two of these strands. To the remaining two pins add one silver-lined crystal bugle and one pale yellow Ceylon seed bead. Trim the wires and form loops, as before.

5 Separate the strands into two identical sets and arrange them from longest to shortest within each set (see page 135 for instructions on opening and closing jump rings). Attach a jump ring to the top of the longest strand in the first set. Twist open a second jump ring and thread it onto the ring at the top of the longest strand and the second longest strand of the set. Close the jump ring.

6 Twist open a third jump ring and thread on the ring you completed in Step 5 and the next longest strand of the set. Close the ring. Repeat to add a fourth ring. Open a fifth ring and thread the ring you just completed onto it, the final strand of the set and the loop of the first earring hook. Close the ring (see figure at right). Assemble the second earring the same way.

# Chain Link Chandeliers

*By Heidi Boyd, from* Simply Beaded Bliss

This earring features an unlikely mix of natural shell, wooden, glass and resin beads strung horizontally onto thin wire. The wire ends hook onto a small length of chain to make unique triangular drop earrings.

## MATERIALS & TOOLS

2—3" (8cm) lengths of small link chain

2—wooden beads

6—apple resin beads

4—teardop shell beads

4—brown foil E beads

4—brown foil seed beads

2—5" (13cm) lengths of 22-gauge silver-plated wire

2—silver-plated earring hooks

2—2" (5cm) eyepins

4—4mm silver-plated jump rings

2—pairs flat- or chain-nose pliers

Round-nose pliers

Chain-nose pliers

Wire cutters

1 Use round-nose pliers to turn a loop in one end of the wire, link the end of the chain into the loop and wrap the loop closed (see page 131 for instructions on creating a wire-wrapped loop). Trim the wire end with wire cutters.

2 Slide each teardrop onto a jump ring, and use pliers to tightly close the rings (see page 135 for instructions on opening and closing jump rings). String beads onto the wire in the following sequence: seed bead, E bead, apple resin bead, teardrop, resin bead, teardrop, resin bead, E bead, seed bead.

3 Shape the free end of the wire into a loop, slide it through the free end of the chain and then wrap the loop closed. Trim away the excess wire with wire cutters.

4 Hook the eyepin into the center link of the chain. Thread a wooden bead onto the eyepin and then make a wrapped loop above the bead. Trim away the excess wire. Add an earring hook to the top of the loop. Repeat Steps 1 through 4 to make a second earring.

# Five Easy Earrings

*By Margot Potter, from* The Impatient Beader Gets Inspired!

Earrings are one of the most quick-to-make and rewarding jewelry projects you can tackle. Here the colors and themes are drawn from lovely art nouveau images. Art nouveau artists were particularly interested in using nature as their source of inspiration, so why not take a cue from them and try venturing outside into the wilds of nature to see what might inspire you!

## *CATHEDRAL DIAMOND CHANDELIER EARRINGS*
## MATERIALS & TOOLS

6—4mm tourmaline Swarovski bicone beads

6—6mm purple velvet Swarovski rondelle beads

2—6mm padparascha Swarovski briolette beads

2—2-section sterling chandelier earring components

2—6mm sterling silver jump rings

12—20-gauge sterling silver headpins

2—sterling silver earring hooks

2—pairs of flat- or chain-nose pliers

Chain-nose pliers

1 To make these long and slender chandelier earrings, simply slide each of the smaller beads onto a headpin and create a loop at the top of each bead (see page 130 for instructions on creating a simple loop).

2 Slide the larger briolette beads onto jump rings.

3 Attach all the beads to the chandelier components as shown. Attach the earring hooks to finish the earrings.

## EARTH FLOWER EARRINGS
### MATERIALS & TOOLS

2—8mm dyed green jade coin beads
2—8mm dyed orange jade coin beads
2—9mm carved dyed blue jade flower beads
2—6mm sterling silver ball beads
6—20-gauge sterling silver headpins
2—star-tipped headpins
2—sterling silver chandelier earring components
2—sterling silver earring hooks

Chain-nose pliers

1  To make these delicate dangles, simply thread each bead onto a headpin and turn a loop at the top (see page 130 for instructions on creating a simple loop).

2  Attach the dangles to the chandelier components as shown.

3  The center sterling silver bead goes on a star-tipped headpin.

4  To create a left and a right earring, make the two earrings mirror images of each other.

5  Attach the components to the earring hooks.

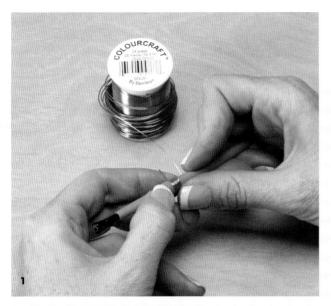

## FILIGREE FLOWER EARRINGS
### MATERIALS & TOOLS

4—5mm × 4mm coral tube beads

2—8mm × 6mm lime green opaque Czech glass oval beads

8—5mm × 6mm eggshell blue Czech glass teardrop beads

2—filigree flower chandelier earring posts

2—20-gauge gold-plated headpins

24-gauge gold-plated craft wire

8mm diameter dowel rod or paintbrush handle

Wire cutters

Chain-nose and round-nose pliers

1 Begin to make jump rings by wrapping wire from the spool around an 8mm paintbrush handle or a dowel rod.

2 Slide the wire off of the paintbrush or dowel rod and use wire cutters to cut the coiled wire from the spool and into jump rings. You'll need to make a total of eight jump rings.

3 Cut off four 1" (3cm) segments of 24-gauge wire with your wire cutters and slide each coral tube onto a length of wire. Make a loop, working at the very end of the pliers

(see page 130 for instructions on creating a simple loop). Make a second larger loop in the wire at the other end of the bead. Make a total of four coral dangles.

4 Make the remaining dangles for each earring: Slide eight eggshell blue teardrops onto gold jump rings and two green Czech glass ovals onto headpins and turn a loop in the wire above them. Lay out all of your components and then use round- and chain-nose pliers to link them to the earring posts.

## GOLD ETRUSCAN BIRDS

### MATERIALS & TOOLS

2—10mm × 8mm faceted dyed purple jade oval beads

4—4mm faceted mint green AB Czech glass round beads

4—6mm striated purple and green Czech glass rondelle beads

2—Etruscan vermeil bird clasps

8—2mm gold-plated jump rings

10—20-gauge gold-plated headpins

2—gold-plated lever-back earring hooks

2—pairs of flat- or chain-nose pliers

Chain-nose pliers

Wire cutters

1 Here I've repurposed a clasp as an earring component. If you use a similar component, you'll need to remove the toggle clasp and jump ring. The jump ring has been soldered, so I had to cut it off with wire cutters.

2 Slide each of the following beads onto headpins and make a wrapped loop in the wire at the top of the bead: two faceted purple jade ovals, four striated purple and green rondelles and four faceted mint green Czech rounds (see page 131 for instructions on creating a wire-wrapped loop). Link each purple jade oval directly to the center loop of the earring component. Slide each dangle onto a jump ring and link the jump rings to the earring components (see page 135 for instructions on opening and closing jump rings). Link an earring hook to the loop at the top of each component to finish.

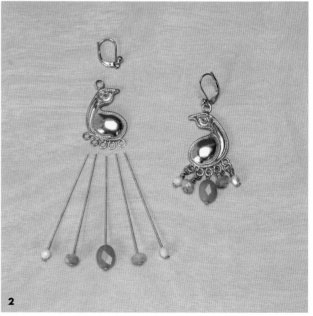

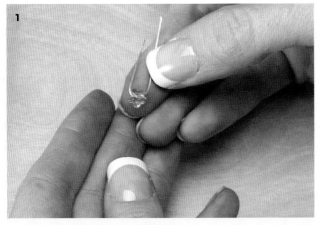

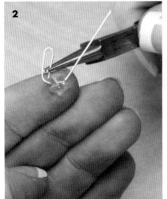

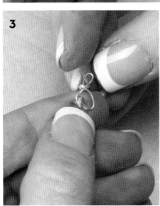

## SEAFARER THREADER EARRINGS

### MATERIALS & TOOLS

2—6mm smoky quartz Swarovski bicone beads

2—6mm erinite Swarovski briolette beads

2—5mm aqua Swarovski side-drilled flower beads

2—20-gauge sterling silver ball-tip headpins

2—20-gauge sterling silver headpins

2—4mm sterling silver jump rings

2—2mm sterling silver jump rings

2—5" (13cm) sterling silver threader earring components

2—pairs of flat- or chain-nose pliers

Round-nose pliers

Wire cutters

1 Slide an aqua flower bead onto a silver headpin and bend the wire into a U shape.

2 Use round-nose pliers to bend one side of the wire back down toward the bead.

3 Wrap the remaining end of the wire around the doubled-up wire to create a loop. Make a second aqua flower dangle for the other earring. Use the wire cutters to clip the excess wire tails.

4 Make the remaining dangles for the earrings, two each of the following: an erinite briolette on a jump ring (see page 135 for instructions on opening and closing jump rings) and a smoky quartz bicone crystal on a headpin with a wrapped loop (see page 131 for instructions on creating a wire-wrapped loop). Attach each set of dangles to a silver jump ring and attach the jump ring to the end loop on the threader earrings.

# Stone and Chain

*By Heidi Boyd, from* Simply Beautiful Beaded Jewelry

A popular trend in earring design has been to hang individual, pairs or small groups of beads from short lengths of chain. The appeal is easy to understand—the finished earrings swing playfully from your earlobes. The key to success is scaling the width and length of the chain to the size of the beads. This design pairs a heavier-weight chain with carved teardrop stones. Experiment to find what works best for you.

## MATERIALS & TOOLS

2—2" (5cm) lengths of sterling silver cable chain

2—teardrop carved fluorite stones

2—2" (5cm) sterling silver eyepins

2—sterling silver earring hooks

Round-nose pliers

Chain-nose pliers

Wire cutters

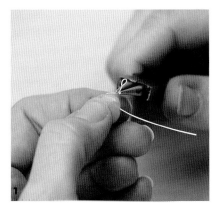

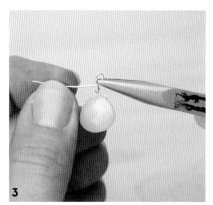

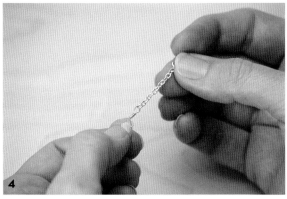

1 Slide a blue fluorite stone onto an eyepin and bend the loop end of the eyepin up to the top of the stone.

2 Bend the other end of the eyepin up to the top of the stone and bring it across the other end of the wire.

3 Wrap the tail end of the wire around the base of the eyepin loop several times to secure the stone. Trim away the excess wire with wire cutters.

4 Open the eyepin loop and slide the dangle onto the last link of a 2" (5cm) section of chain. Close the link with round- and chain-nose pliers.

5 Attach the top link of the chain to an earring hook loop and close the link with pliers. Repeat Steps 1 through 5 to make a second earring.

# Sun and Sea Swing

*By Sara Schwittek, from* Perfect Match

You can almost feel the warmth from the sun's rays radiating from the gold chains in this design. The delicate swaying chains allow the faceted zircon to rock buoyantly like the waves on the ocean. The faceted orange carnelian makes subtle references to the sun in the sky.

## MATERIALS & TOOLS

2–3–4mm faceted carnelian beads

12–4mm zircon faceted beads

1–18" (46cm) length of gold-filled chain, delicate links

1–5" (13cm) length of 26-gauge half-hard gold-filled wire

12–1½" (4cm) gold-filled headpins

2–gold-filled earring hooks

Round-nose pliers

Wire cutters

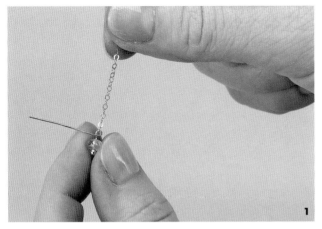

1 Cut twelve pieces of chain approximately 1½" (4cm) long (count the links of each piece if you want to make sure they're all exactly the same length). To create the dangle on the chain tassels, insert a headpin into a zircon bead. Begin to make a wire-wrapped loop and insert the last link on the chain before wrapping it two or three times to close (see page 131 for instructions on creating a wire-wrapped loop). Repeat for each piece of chain.

2 With about 2½" (6cm) of wire, create an open loop. Insert six chains into the loop before securing it closed with two or three wraps.

3 Slide a carnelian bead onto the tail of the wire and make a wire-wrapped loop at the top of the bead. Connect the earring hook to the top loop and repeat Steps 2 and 3 to create the second earring.

# Teal and Crystal

*By Carole Rodgers, from* Beading Basics

Swarovski crystals provide the glitter in this pair of chandelier earrings.

## MATERIALS & TOOLS

6—9mm × 6mm clear AB faceted crystal beads

12—6mm teal AB bicone crystal beads

32—4mm Bali sterling silver daisy spacer beads

4—3mm × 5mm Bali sterling silver spacer beads

10—3mm sterling silver round beads

2—2½" (6cm) Bali sterling silver headpins

4—2" (5cm) Bali sterling silver headpins

2—sterling silver three-hole-to-one findings

10—4mm sterling silver jump rings

2—sterling silver earring hooks

2—pairs of flat- or chain-nose pliers

Round-nose pliers

Wire cutters

1 Thread beads onto one 2" (5cm) headpin in the following sequence: daisy, teal, daisy, clear, daisy, teal, daisy, round, daisy, round. (See Figure 1.)

2 Turn the end of the pin into a wrapped loop (see page 131 for instructions on creating a wire-wrapped loop).

3 Repeat Steps 1 and 2 with the remaining three 2" (5cm) headpins. Set all four pins aside.

4 Thread beads onto a 2½" (6cm) headpin in the following sequence: daisy, teal, daisy, Bali spacer, daisy, clear, daisy, Bali spacer, daisy, teal, daisy, round. (See Figure 2.)

5 Repeat Step 4 for the other 2½" (6cm) headpin.

6 Use jump rings to attach each 2½" (6cm) beaded headpin to the center loop of each three-hole finding (see page 135 for instructions on opening and closing jump rings).

7 Use jump rings to attach each 2" (5cm) beaded headpin to the outside loops of each three-hole finding.

8 Use jump rings to attach the top loop of each earring finding to each earring hook. You may need two jump rings per finding to get the earrings to hang correctly.

Figure 1.　　Figure 2.

# 3

# Intermediate Earrings

The projects in this chapter go a step further. Many of the same skills are used for these projects as those found in Chapter 2, but they each require a bit more care and attention. However, in return for care and attention, the extra steps you see here will allow you to customize your earrings, try new techniques, or practice techniques you may not have used in a while. As you dive into this chapter, get ready to make your own earring hooks, hoops and more!

If you'd like to learn how to make a traditional earring hook, check out the *Shepherd's Hooks* earrings on page 58. These easy earrings are elevated by their handmade hooks. For a nontraditional, striking earring hook, the *Effortless Elegance* earrings on page 52 are perfect. The swooping, dramatic line created by the hand-formed earring hook adds punch to the look of this pair. Try the *Bombay Hoops* on page 64 to learn not only how to make your own hoop, but also how to wrap it in shining metal and sparkling beads. To give a familiar material new use, try using bead-stringing wire to make the *Luxurious Loops* earrings on page 70 or the *Cascade* earrings on page 74. Bead-stringing wire, a staple of necklaces and bracelets, isn't usually featured in earrings, but these projects show off a material that is usually hidden in jewelry. The projects on these pages are sure to introduce you to something new!

QUEEN ANNE'S LACE *by Margot Potter*
*To learn how to make these earrings, see page 72.*

# Effortless Elegance

*By Margot Potter, from* Bead Chic

There could be nothing simpler than these bent-wire earrings with beaded dangles, and yet they're fascinating. It's easy to make your own earring hooks, and you can endlessly play with scale and shape and embellishments. You'll be mad for these; plan to make them in a rainbow of colors!

## MATERIALS & TOOLS

2—12mm × 17mm black onyx polished teardrop beads

6—3mm red coral beads

6—1½" (4cm) 24-gauge sterling silver headpins

2—2" (5cm) ball tip sterling silver headpins

2—3" (7cm) segments of 20-gauge sterling silver wire

Thin metal dowel (the metal end of a rattail comb was used here)

Sanding block

Round-nose pliers

Chain-nose pliers

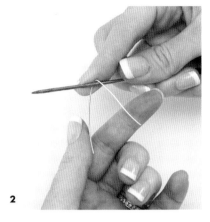

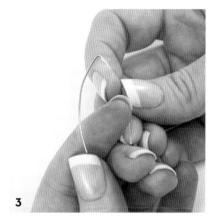

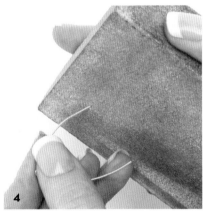

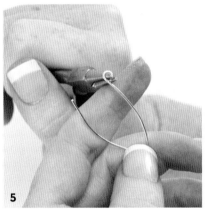

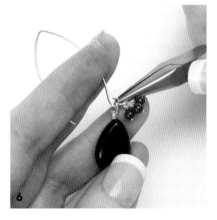

1 Cut two 3" (8cm) segments of wire.

2 Bend each wire segment (not quite in the center of the wire) over the thin dowel and create a crease or point. Make sure the crease is in the same spot on both wires.

3 Gently round both wire tails into matching curves.

4 Using the sanding block, sand the ends of the wires.

5 Bend a loop in one end of each piece of the wire, using the round-nose pliers (see page 130 for instructions on creating a simple loop).

6 Create wrapped dangles using the ball tip headpins and onyx beads (see page 133 for instructions on making a looped dangle). Repeat for the coral beads using regular headpins. Using the chain-nose pliers to open and close the loop at the end of each wire, attach the beads to the loop, onyx dangle first, followed by the three coral dangles.

# Japanese Crosses

*By Rebeca Mojica, from Chained*

This pattern was one of the first earring designs I created, and it quickly became one of my most popular designs. After you learn the basic pattern, have fun by varying the colors, linking additional components or adding beads. As you'll see on the next few pages, the possibilities are endless!

## MATERIALS & TOOLS

14—large jump rings: K16 copper 16 gauge, $^{15}/_{64}$" (6.0mm)

20—small jump rings: F19 enameled copper 19 gauge, $^{5}/_{32}$" (4.0mm):

> 16—seafoam color
>
> 4—gunmetal color

2—earring hooks

2—pairs of flat-nose pliers

small piece of wire (optional)

1 To prepare, close the small rings and open the large rings (see page 135 for instructions on opening and closing jump rings). Use an open large copper ring to scoop four seafoam and two gunmetal closed enameled copper rings. Close the open ring.

2 Double the copper ring by taking a new open copper ring and weaving it through the same six closed small rings.

3 Using a new open large copper ring, scoop four seafoam rings and then weave the open copper ring through the two gunmetal rings from Step 1. Close the copper ring.

4 To double the copper ring added in Step 3, use a new open copper ring to go through all six small rings that the ring from Step 3 went through. Most people find it easier to go through the two gunmetal ones first because they are tighter and more fixed in place, and then go through the four seafoam rings. Close the copper ring.

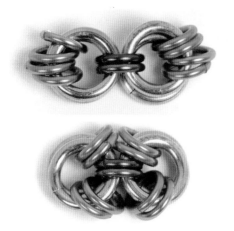

**5**

**6**

**7**

**8**

5 To prepare for the next step, pull two pairs of seafoam rings—one pair from each copper unit—up toward each other. Use a piece of wire to move the rings if it helps.

6 Take a new open large copper ring and weave it through those two sets of small seafoam rings. You'll go through four rings total. Close the ring.

7 Double the last ring by going through all four small rings with a new large ring.

8 On the other side of the weave, pull the remaining four hanging seafoam rings toward one another, then go through them with a new copper ring. Before closing the large ring, add the earring hook. The ring that connects to the earring hook is not doubled. Normally, it would be doubled, but the loop on most earring hooks is not large enough to accommodate two thick 16-gauge rings. After the last large ring is closed, you're done with one earring! Repeat Steps 1-8 to create the second earring.

# Japanese Cross Variations

Making a few tiny changes, such as swapping ring sizes or adding beads, makes a world of difference in these variations. Try each one for a completely new look!

*You can easily vary one or all of the colors in this weave to suit your tastes.*

## Mini Japanese Crosses

*The pattern here is almost identical to the Japanese Cross; the only differences are that the ring connected to the earring hook is doubled in this mini version, while the ring connected to the crystal is not—it is a single ring. Using smaller rings does make this pair of earrings more challenging.*

## Doubled Mini Japanese Crosses

*This variation uses tiny sterling silver rings to link multiple crosses together.*

# Shepherd's Hooks

*By Sharilyn Miller, from* Bead on a Wire

Combine your favorite charms or bead dangles with a simple shepherd's hook earring, and you have a five-minute piece of jewelry! These earrings provide the opportunity to show off some favorite beads or charms, so take the time to select a nice combination of beads, bead caps and decorative headpins for the bead dangles.

## MATERIALS & TOOLS

Assorted beads, bead caps and/or pearls in various sizes and colors

20- or 22-gauge round wire

Wire cutters

Chain-nose pliers

Small round-nose pliers

Extra-long round-nose pliers

Bent-nose pliers

Hard plastic mallet

Steel block

Chasing hammer

Needle file

0000 steel wool

Liver-of-sulfur solution (optional)

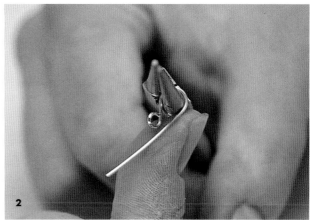

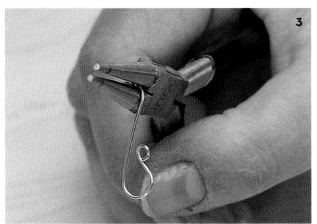

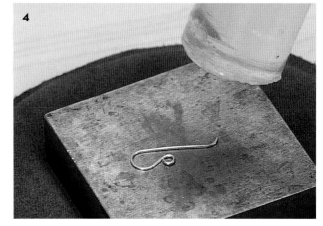

To Get Started: Select an assortment of beads, bead caps and headpins for the bead dangles. For the earring hooks, cut two lengths of 22-gauge (preferred) or 20-gauge wire, each measuring 4", 3" or 2" (10cm, 8cm or 5cm), depending on how long you want your earring hooks to be. Then:

1 Make two bead dangles with decorative headpins and bead caps (see page 133 for instructions on making looped dangles). After they are assembled, set them aside.

2 On one end of each wire length, create a single loop in the middle of the small round-nose pliers. Grip the wire directly under the loop and make another loop at the back of the extra-long round-nose pliers, as shown.

3 Place the straight end of the looped wire in the back of the extra-long round-nose pliers and make a tiny bend in the last ⅛" (3mm) of the wire. Repeat with the other looped wire.

4 Hammer each earring hook with a hard plastic mallet on a steel block.

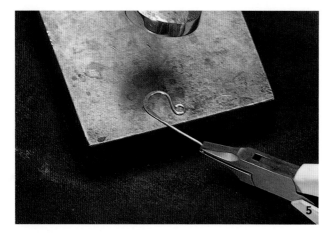

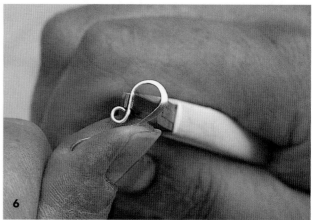

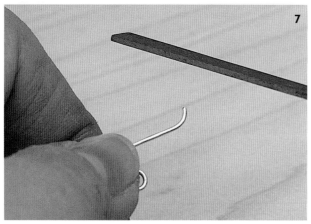

5 Use a chasing hammer to flatten the rounded part of each earring hook.

6 Use pliers to pull the rounded part of each earring hook back into shape.

7 File the end of each earring hook. Be sure to file in one direction only. Polish with 0000 steel wool.

8 Open the earring loops sideways and slip one bead dangle onto each wire. Close the loops to secure. After they are assembled, you can artificially age your earrings in a liver-of-sulfur solution if desired.

# Variation: Hook Earrings

This is simply a different way to make Shepherd's Hooks. In this variation, you add the bead dangle as you shape the wire instead of first forming the loop and then attaching the dangle. See pages 62-63 for detailed instructions to create these earring variations.

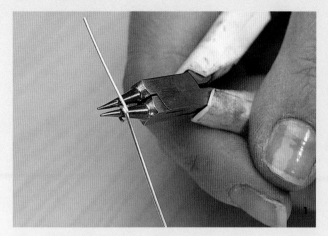

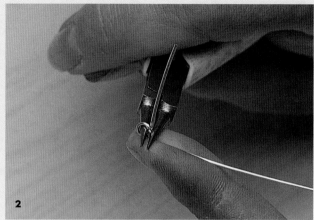

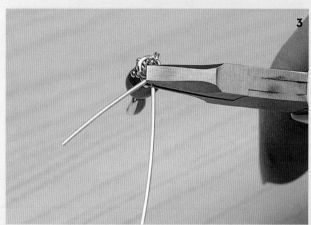

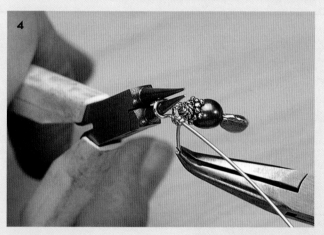

To Get Started: Select an assortment of beads, bead caps and headpins, and then make bead dangles. For the earrings, cut two 4" (10cm) lengths of 20-gauge wire. If you want shorter earring hooks, adjust the length to 3" (8cm) or 3½" (9cm).

1 Use the small round-nose pliers to grip one of the lengths of wire 1" (3mm) from the end of the wire. While gripping the pliers, roll your wrist forward to create a loop.

2 Insert the round-nose pliers into the loop as far as it will go. Place the wire on your index finger as shown. Then push your right wrist forward abruptly to break the neck. You have just created an eyepin.

3 Open the eyepin and place the bead dangle on it. With the pliers, squeeze the eyepin to close it.

4 Insert the small round-nose pliers into the eyepin to hold the wire steady. Use the bent-nose pliers to wrap the short tail of the wire around the length three times at the base of the eyepin.

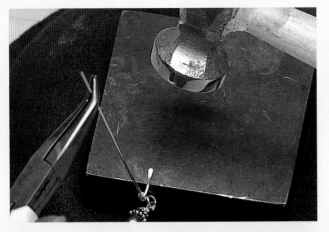

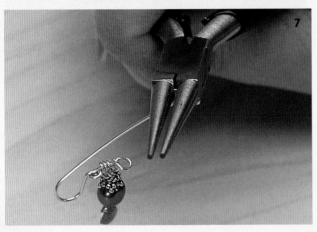

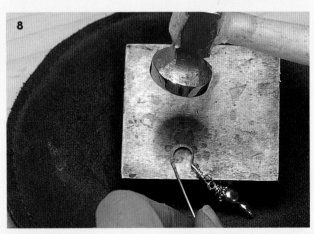

5 Use a chasing hammer to flatten only the short tail remaining from the wrapped wire, as shown. After it's flat, spiral the wire tail in and tuck it against the straight wire.

6 Place the wire in the back of the extra-long round-nose pliers with the bead dangle hanging beneath the pliers. Then bend the wire up and over the tool to create a loop.

7 With the extra-long round-nose pliers, bend the last ¼" (6mm) of wire just slightly. File the end smooth. Polish with 0000 steel wool. Make the second earring, repeating Steps 1 through 7.

8 Use a chasing hammer to flatten the rounded top of each earring wire. After they are assembled, you can artificially age your earrings in a liver-of-sulfur solution if desired.

# Bombay Hoops

*By Sara Schwittek, from* Perfect Match

Experiment with colors and textures for the beads in this design; virtually any rounded bead measuring 3mm or 4mm will work. This design doesn't require a separate earring hook. One end of the hoop slides directly through the earlobe. Use a smaller mandrel for petite earrings or a larger mandrel for adventurously bold hoops!

## MATERIALS & TOOLS

1—10" (25cm) length of 20- or 21-gauge half-hard gold-filled wire

1—32" (81cm) length of 26- or 28-gauge half-hard gold-filled wire

22—3mm garnet faceted round beads

1" (3cm) diameter mandrel

Wire cutters

Chain-nose pliers

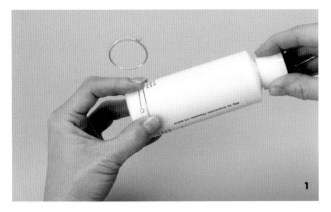

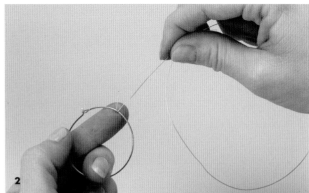

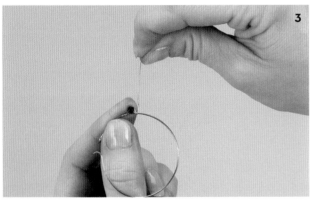

1 Using the 20- or 21-gauge wire, create two earring hoops approximately 1½" (4cm) in diameter. You can use a mandrel or just about any round object to create the diameter you want. You can also use premade hoops.

2 To wrap the beads, cut about 16" (41cm) of 26- or 28-gauge half-hard wire (for 1½" [4cm] hoops). With about ½" (13mm) tail, hold the wire at about the 2 o'clock mark on the hoop and coil the short tail of the wire up toward the top of the hoop with your fingers. Wrap the tail around five or six times, then cut. Tuck the sharp end down with the chain-nose pliers. Keep the coil steady by holding it with the chain-nose pliers.

3 After the coil is secure onto the hoop, thread one of the garnet beads on the free, long end of the wire. Hold the

garnet in one hand securely on the outside ridge of the hoop. With the other hand, continue to coil the wire around the hoop in the same direction as you started. Coil around as closely as possible without overlapping or leaving gaps. If there is a gap, squeeze the coils together with your fingernails until the gap closes.

4 Repeat Step 3 with ten more garnet beads until the coiling is symmetrical to the starting point on the other side (10 o'clock). Remember to leave enough space in the front of the hoop to accommodate your earlobe! Cut the end of the wire at the last coil and press any sharp edges in with the chain-nose pliers. Repeat with the other hoop.

# Hoop Earrings Your Way

*By Sharilyn Miller, from* Bead on a Wire

Hoop earrings are a jewelry box staple that never go out of style, and you can alter the look easily by adding your favorite beads and dangling charms. Found objects—anything from small game pieces to metal scraps from other jewelry projects (all edges filed smooth!)—are especially fun to place on hoop earrings. Try anything you find that has an interesting line, shape, color or texture.

## MATERIALS & TOOLS

20-gauge round wire

Wire cutters

Round-nose pliers

Flat-nose pliers

Various mandrels (or markers or large wooden dowels) in different sizes for forming hoops

Chasing hammer

Steel block

Hard plastic mallet

Needle file or sanding block

Liver-of-sulfur solution (optional)

Embellishments such as beads, charms, bead dangles, predrilled found objects, coiled bead wraps and other items (optional)

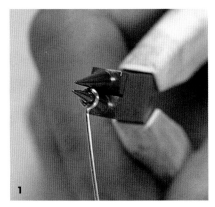
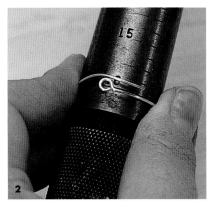
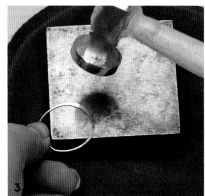
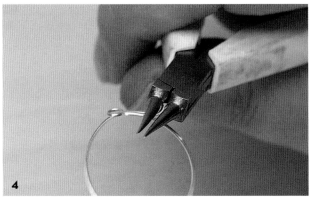

1 Cut two pieces of 20-gauge wire to the desired length, which will depend on how large you want the hoops to be. A good starting point for your first pair would be about 4" (10cm). Make sure both wire pieces are exactly the same length. Make a simple loop on one end of each length of wire (see page 130 for instructions on creating simple loops).

2 At this point you will need a smooth, round mandrel; you can also use a fat marker, a ring mandrel or a large wooden dowel. Wrap each wire around the mandrel to form a round or oval shape.

3 Hammer the wire with a hard plastic mallet on a steel block to preserve the shape you've created. Then, flatten the bottom portion of each hoop with a chasing hammer.

4 After you are satisfied with the design, grip the straight end of one earring in the middle of the round-nose pliers and bend it up in a slight curve. Repeat with the other earring hook.

5 Grip the loop with the flat-nose pliers and bend it straight up, perpendicular to the hoop, as shown. The curved end should hook right onto the loop. File the end of the wire very smooth (see the tip on the next page). Repeat for the other earring. Once assembled, you can artificially age your earrings in a liver-of-sulfur solution.

# Variation: Embellished Earrings

You can add beads, charms, bead dangles, coiled-wire wraps or other items to your wire hoops. Follow Steps 1 and 2 as instructed on the previous page. Then, hammer the hoops with only the hard plastic mallet. Do not flatten the hoop. Continue with one of the following steps (or one of your own), and then finish the earrings with Steps 4 and 5. When choosing beads, charms or found objects, select lightweight items that won't drag on your earlobes.

## Add beads and bead dangles

Slip your choice of beads and bead dangles directly onto the straight end of the wire.

## Add a coiled-bead wrap

Slip a single- or double-coiled bead wrap directly onto the straight end of the wire.

# Tips

*It's important to file the wire end until it is very smooth because, as it passes through the pierced tissue of your earlobe, any sharp edges could create micro-tears in your skin, resulting in inflammation. Always file in one direction and, when finished, rub the wire end briskly with 0000 steel wool.*

*Allergic to metals? Apply a thin coat of clear nail polish to the wire where it passes through your earlobe to alleviate any problems.*

# Variation: Rectangle Earrings

Rectangular in shape, these earrings are made using the same general technique as the hoops. It's easy to create your own variation with ovals, squares or even triangles.

1 To get started, cut two pieces of 20-gauge wire to 4¾" (12cm). You can make the length shorter for smaller earrings or longer for larger earrings. Then make a simple loop on one end of each length of wire (see page 130 for instructions on creating simple loops). Hold one loop lengthwise along a ruler. At 1½" (4cm), use the flat-nose pliers to bend the wire at a 90-degree angle. Repeat for the other loop.

2 Measure ½" (13mm) from the first bend and then bend the wire back up. Hammer the wire with a hard plastic mallet if it's crooked.

3 Slip a coiled-wire bead wrap, bead dangles or any other accent pieces onto the straight end of the wire. Slide the pieces into the desired position on each earring.

4 Measure 1½" (4cm) of the remaining length and then bend the wire toward the loop to complete the rectangle. The straight end should fit through the loop. File the end of the wire very smooth. If desired, artificially age the earrings.

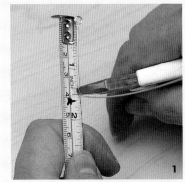
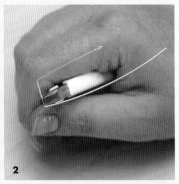

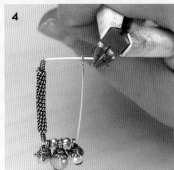

# Luxurious Loops

*By Fernando Dasilva, from* Modern Expressions

These glamorous and femme fatale earrings are so easy to make, you'll want to make a pair for everyone you know. They are perfect for wearing to a wedding, a prom or a ball at the White House . . . hey, you never know; it could happen! These earrings will add equal elegance to a flowery summer dress or a satin ball gown.

## MATERIALS & TOOLS

1—24" (61cm) length of 19-strand .018" blue stringing wire (Beadalon)

2—#4 silver-plated crimp tubes

2—7mm silver-plated sparkle crimp covers

2—6mm silver-plated jump rings

2—back loop earring hooks

1—5" (13cm) length of Swarovski Elements aquamarine Crystal mesh

2—pairs of flat- or chain-nose pliers

Chain-nose pliers

Wire cutters

Crimping tool

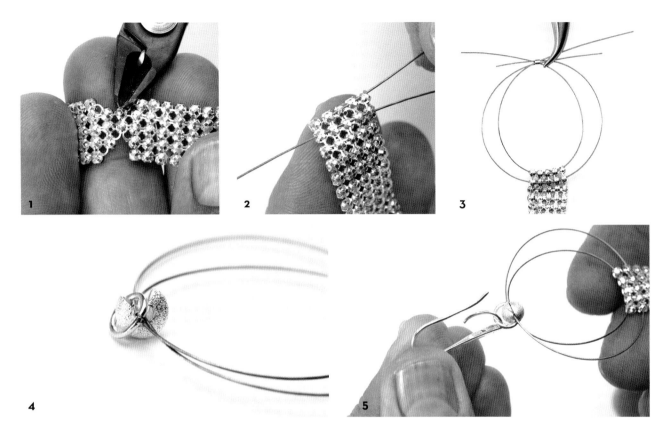

1 Using wire cutters, cut a piece of aquamarine mesh into a 5 stone × 17 stone rectangle. Trim around the rectangle to create clean edges, cutting carefully so the back prongs are not damaged. Cut one of the five-stone ends into a triangular point and then trim again to create clean edges.

2 Carefully thread a 6" (15cm) piece of blue stringing wire through the remaining five-stone end of the rectangle. Thread a second 6" (15cm) piece of blue wire through the row of five stones directly below. Center both wires on the rectangle.

3 Curve the left ends of the two wires up and into a crimp tube. Do the same with the right ends, going through the opposite side of the same crimp tube so the two left wires intersect with the two right wires inside the tube. Adjust the wires to form a smaller circle inside of a slightly larger circle and then crimp the tube.

4 Trim the ends of the wires at the crimp tube. Cover the crimp tube with a sparkle crimp cover, but before closing, place a jump ring into the crimp cover. Use a crimping tool to close the crimp cover with the crimp tube and the jump ring inside.

5 Open the loop on an earring hook and slide on the jump ring within the crimp cover. Close the loop. Repeat Steps 1 through 5 to make a matching earring.

# Queen Anne's Lace

*By Margot Potter, from* Bead Chic

Not for the shy or retiring, these earrings will get you noticed! Wire and beads are loosely wrapped along the edge of a brushed metal frame while a large, soft-finish acrylic bead with a floral image is accented with a Quick Links circle. These are fun and flirty, a breeze to create and full of swingy movement when worn.

## MATERIALS & TOOLS

2—Plaid Fresh red acrylic pendants with floral designs

2—Plaid Fresh brushed metal round frames

2—1" (3cm) Quick Links rounds

14—4mm black onyx rounds

22-gauge German-style wire

2—earring hooks

6—6mm jump rings

Round-nose pliers

2—pairs of chain-nose pliers

Wire cutters

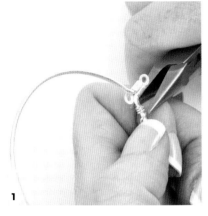

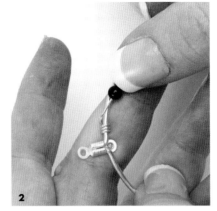

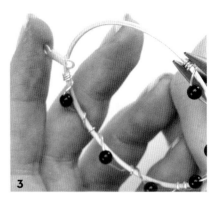

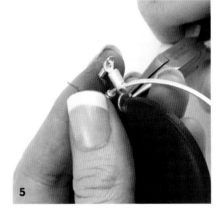

1   Start wrapping one round frame at the top left side with the wire. Tuck the tail under with chain-nose pliers.

2   Make three tight coils and then string on the first bead. This is a looser wrap, so stretch it out a little.

3   Wrap the wire around the frame twice, with enough tension to secure the bead to the front of the frame,

and add the next bead. Continue until you reach the seventh bead. The wire should not go all the way around the frame.

4   Cut the wire and tuck the tail under. Repeat Steps 1 through 4 for the other earring, beginning at the top right side. Attach the earring wires to the tops of the frames.

5   Attach a pendant to the bottom of one of the frame bails using a jump ring (see page 135 for instructions on opening and closing jump rings).

6   Use two jump rings to create a chain and add the Quick Link to the bottom ring. Repeat Steps 5 and 6 for the matching earring.

# Cascade

*by Margot Potter, from* Bead & Wire Jewelry Exposed

The exposed wire tendrils of these earrings explode out of the cones, like a fireworks display, and the beaded wire fringe is a fun take on a traditional idea. This is a the-more-the-merrier situation: The more cones you made, the better the earrings became.

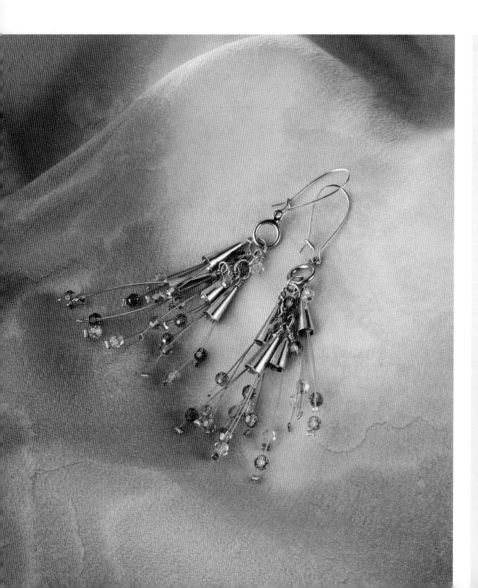

## MATERIALS & TOOLS

10—4mm padparascha crystal round beads

10—4mm Indian sapphire crystal round beads

10—4mm light topaz crystal round beads

10—4mm black diamond AB crystal round beads

8—gold-plated cones

8—2" (5cm) gold-plated eyepins

8—2" (5cm) gold-plated headpins

2—gold-plated kidney-shaped earring wires

32—gold-plated crimp beads

4—5mm gold-plated jump rings

2—small gold-plated toggle circle ends

.018" (0.46mm) Satin Gold wire

Crimp tool

Round-nose pliers

2—pairs flat- or chain-nose pliers

Wire cutters

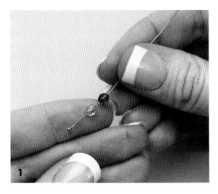
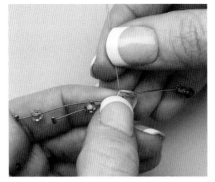
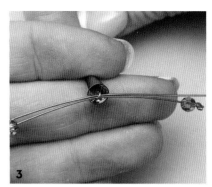

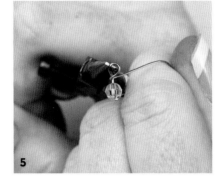
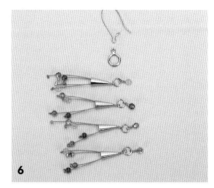

1 Cut eight 3" (8cm) segments and eight 2½" (6cm) segments of Satin Gold wire. Flatten a crimp bead flush to the end of a wire section using the chain-nose pliers. Slide a light topaz and a padparascha bead onto the wire. Flatten a crimp bead flush to the open end of the wire. Cut off excess wire. Repeat to make another beaded segment with an Indian sapphire and a black diamond bead. Make a total of eight padparascha and light topaz beaded segments and eight Indian sapphire and black diamond beaded segments.

2 Thread two beaded segments—one padparascha-topaz and one sapphire-diamond—onto the pre-opened end of an eyepin.

3 Close the eyepin and thread it into a cone. Keep the wires even as you pull the tail of the eyepin inside the cone, using round-nose pliers to grab the wire.

4 Keep tension on the eyepin as you create a wire-wrapped loop at the top of the cone (see page 131 for instructions on creating a wrapped-wire loop). Using the wire you cut in Step 1, repeat Steps 1 through 4 to make fringe with four cones for each earring, creating two cones for each earring with short tassels and two with long tassels.

5 Slide each of the remaining beads (two of each color) onto headpins and make a wrapped loop above each bead.

6 Slide one dangle and one cone onto a jump ring (see page 135 for instructions on opening and closing jump rings). Repeat for the remaining cones and dangles. Link four jump rings together in a chain, and then link the top jump ring to a toggle clasp ring. Link the ring to an earring hook. Repeat to make the second earring.

# Crystal Balls

*By Heidi Boyd, from* Simply Beaded Bliss

Swarovski packs a whole lot of sparkle into one little bead. So when you wire them together into a ball, you end up with an incredibly eye-catching earring or pendant. The best part is that it isn't as complicated as it looks. Sets of three beads are strung onto the wire and wrapped around the outside of a core bead. When all is said and done, what you'll see is sparkle on all fronts.

## MATERIALS & TOOLS

2—9mm × 6mm ruby Swarovski crystal oval beads

40—4mm ruby Swarovski crystal bicone beads

40—ruby seed beads

2—13" (33cm) lengths of 32-gauge beading wire

2—3" (8cm) lengths of .018" (.46mm) stringing wire

1—pair of lever-back earring hooks

2—2" (5cm) thin silver headpins

4—silver crimp beads

Wire cutters

Round-nose pliers

Chain-nose pliers

1 Form a loop around the oval bead: Thread the 32-gauge wire through an oval bead, pulling it through so 1" to 1¹/₂" (3cm to 4cm) extends beyond the top of the bead. Thread three bicone beads onto the long end of the wire. Bring the beaded wire up against the side of the oval bead and thread the wire end down through the top of the bead (where the wire end extends). The beaded wire will form a loop around the oval bead, holding the bicones against the oval bead. Pull the wire tight so the bicones rest against the side of the oval bead.

2 Repeat Step 1 to make two more beaded loops. Three loops form half of the crystal ball.

3 Make three more wraps to completely cover the core bead. Thread the beading wire up through three wrapped beads to bring it up next to the short wire end, twist the wires together, trim the ends and poke the twisted wire inside a bicone bead.

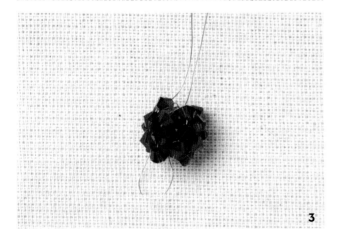

4 Thread a 4mm bicone onto the headpin, then thread the pin up through the center of the finished crystal ball, and thread on one more 4mm bicone. Create a wrapped loop above the beads (see page 131 for instructions on creating a wire-wrapped loop).

5 Thread a 3" (8cm) length of .018 wire through the headpin loop and bring a short tail through the loop. Thread a crimp bead onto both wires and squeeze the crimp bead flat to secure the wire.

6 String 20 seed beads (about 1½" [4cm]) and a crimp bead onto the wire. Bring the wire end through the opening in the earring hook, pass it back down through the crimp and pull it tight to remove any slack. Flatten the bead with chain-nose pliers. Repeat Steps 1 through 6 to create a second earring.

## Variation: Crystal Ball Necklace

To make this gleaming necklace (which can be made in any color you desire—match the earrings or go for a whole different look!), follow the same steps as for the earrings to make the crystal pendant, and then slide it onto the center of a simple beaded strand.

## Tip

If you're having trouble locating the specified core bead, substitute an oblong glass bead. You may also use a different sized bead and adapt the number of crystals wrapped around the sides as necessary.

# Golden Glow

*By Fernando Dasilva, from* Bead & Wire Jewelry Exposed

My mother never goes out in public without at least a pair of earrings. I know there are many women like her, and that led me to envision a pair of slim and elegant drop earrings suitable for many occasions. In this design, I paired polished surfaces with rubber textures. The result is an updated version of the traditional drop earring—an edgy but wearable design.

## MATERIALS & TOOLS

2—24mm × 12mm Terrenum long crystal teardrop pendants

2—14mm light Colorado topaz square crystal buttons

24-gauge gold-plated German-style wire

14—4mm gold-plated lightweight jump rings

2—6mm gold-plated jump rings

2—gold-plated modern earring hooks

6—gold-plated pinch bails

58—1.7mm satin gold cube Bead Bumpers

2—pairs of flat- or chain-nose pliers

Round-nose pliers

Crimp tool

Wire cutters

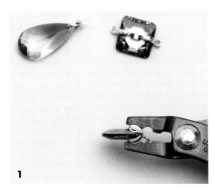

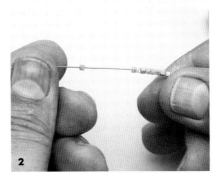

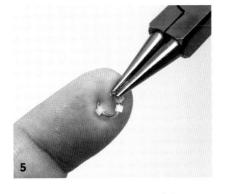

1 Slide a pinch bail into the hole in the long teardrop crystal. Squeeze the pinch bail closed using the outside jaw of the crimp tool. Use gentle pressure to avoid chipping the crystal. Secure two pinch bails to the square button, bringing each pinch bail through the center hole and again using gentle pressure with the crimp tool to close the pinch bails.

2 String 25 satin gold Bead Bumpers onto approximately 4" (10cm) of gold-plated German-style wire.

3 Bend the tip of one end of the wire strung with Bead Bumpers into a U shape. Slide this wire onto the pinch bail the exits the narrow end of the teardrop pendant and bend the end of the wire into a loop (see page 130 for instructions on creating a simple loop). Trim away the excess wire tail with wire cutters.

4 Wrap the beaded wire vertically around the teardrop and then tightly wrap the wire around the pinch bail several times to secure. Trim away excess wire.

5 Open a 6mm round jump ring and string four Bead Bumpers onto it. Close the ring (see page 135 for instructions on opening and closing jump rings).

6 Link the teardrop to the square crystal with two 4mm gold jump rings. Link the beaded jump ring to the top of the square with two more 4mm jump rings. Slide a single 4mm jump ring through the hole in the earring finding. Link the beaded jump ring to the earring hook with two final jump rings. Repeat Steps 1 through 6 to make the second earring.

# Pendulum

*By Fernando Dasilva, from* Modern Expressions

Wire wrapping is one of the most popular jewelry-making techniques. The goal in designing these earrings was to create a fresh design employing wire wrapping. This project explores the geometry of the focal crystal bead, with the wire sculpted around its lines. The result is an almost hoop-style earring with lots of movement and drama.

## MATERIALS & TOOLS

2—Paula Radke Dichroic 6mm cobalt blue dichroic disc beads

2—18mm Swarovski Elements indicolite graphic beads

2—4mm silver-plated jump rings

1—36" (91cm) length of 22-gauge silver-plated German-style wire

2—silver-plated oval hinged ear posts

Chain-nose pliers

Round-nose pliers

Wire cutters

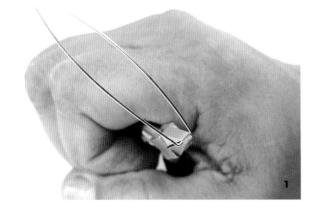

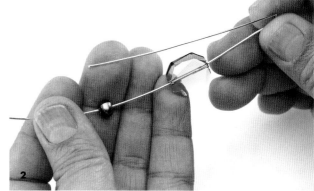

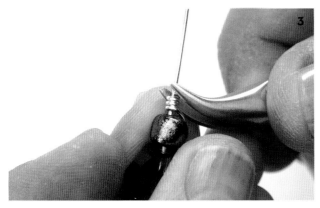

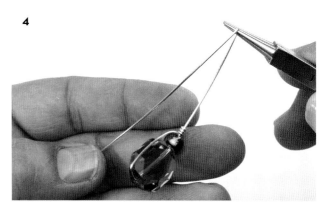

1 Cut a 9" (23cm) piece of German-style wire. Using the chain-nose pliers, pinch the wire about 3" (8cm) from the end. Bend the wire at the pliers to form a U shape.

2 String a graphic bead and a dichroic bead onto the longer portion of the wire.

3 Carefully bend the short portion of the wire up along the side of the graphic bead and the dichroic bead. Wrap the shorter portion of wire around the longer portion tightly, making three full revolutions (see page 134 for instructions on wrapping wire around a base). Trim the excess wire and tuck in the end.

4 Using the round-nose pliers, grasp the longer portion of the wire about 1½" (4cm) above the dichroic bead. Bend the wire at the pliers, making the bend wide enough to attach a 4mm jump ring to it.

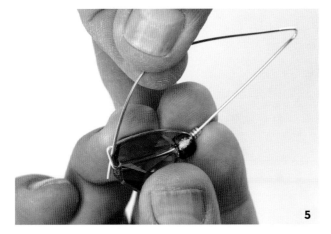

**5** Carefully slide the end of the wire through the bent wire at the bottom of the graphic bead. Bend the wire upward and away from the bead at a 45-degree angle.

**6** Using the round-nose pliers, grasp the wire where it extends from the bent wire. Carefully wrap the wire around one tip of the pliers, forming an upside-down corkscrew. Wrap the wire around the tip four full revolutions. Remove the pliers and cut the excess wire. Close the corkscrew by squeezing it top to bottom with the chain-nose pliers until each corkscrew revolution is flush with the next.

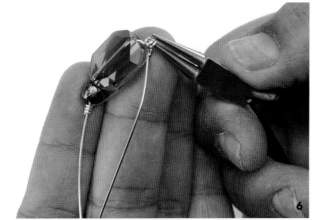

**7** Squeeze the top bend in the earring slightly, using the tip of the round-nose pliers, to accommodate the ear post. Attach a jump ring to the top of the earring. Attach a hinged ear post to the jump ring. Repeat Steps 1 through 7 to make a second earring.

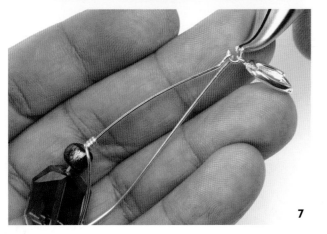

# Fernando Dasilva's Best Tips and Tricks

*(From Modern Expressions)*

"It's time to shine! Jewelry has become one of the most powerful expressions of personal style, and in answer to today's intense quest for individuality, Swarovski Elements, Swarovski's product brand for cut crystal components, fulfills the desire in all of us to create our own personal crystal style. This extensive collection of crystal beads, pendants, trims and more is enhanced and updated twice a year and comes in many shapes, sizes, colors and effects. These earrings can be assembled with any crystal brand of your preference, but I believe that only Swarovski Elements produces maximum light refraction and perfection in cut, luxury and prestige that suits my design ambitions. The use of crystals in the do-it-yourself jewelry market is an affordable way to add bling to complement an outfit. It's instant glamour!"

~Fernando

## Tip

*When working with new wire techniques, it's a good idea to practice wrapping the wire before working with the gemstones. Do not bend the wire too close to the hole in the gemstone, because this may cause it to fracture. Consider using clear bead bumpers on the ends where you have to bend the wire. These will provide some "give" so the hole in the gemstone doesn't have to.*

*4*

# Advanced Earrings

If you're ready for a challenge, take a peek inside this chapter—it's chock-full of projects with surprising twists and turns. If you like molding wire to form your own unique shapes, try the *Snow Queen* earrings on page 96. To take wire work a step further, the *Peas in a Pod* earrings on page 92 offer even more; not only do you shape your wire, you add texture to it as well through hammering. And if you're not looking for the curves you'll find in those earrings, take a sharp turn toward the *Suspended Coral* earrings on page 104 and try shaping wire with right angles.

Wire work isn't the only technique you can try in this chapter. If you've ever wanted to try beadweaving, the *Persephone* earrings on page 114 are a beautiful introduction to this fascinating craft. The *Beaded Bead* earrings on page 110 also let you practice your beadweaving skills. And if you didn't get enough chain mail in Chapters 2 and 3, this chapter ends with the intricate-looking (but still approachable) *Japanese Diamonds* earrings on page 122. Expand your skills and your earring wardrobe with the beautiful projects in this chapter.

DECO CHIC *by Fernanado Dasilva*
*To learn how to make these earrings, see page 118.*

# Hammered

*By Margot Potter, from* Beyond the Bead

Hammering metal is quite a simple technique, and after you start pounding a small hammer on a tiny anvil and making hammered metal links and squiggles, all of the cares of your day-to-day world simply slip away. It's a great way to get out your aggression and make stylish jewelry, all at the same time.

## MATERIALS & TOOLS

20-gauge copper wire

Selection of assorted crystals (3 for each earring)

8—5mm copper jump rings

Mini anvil or steel block

Mini chasing hammer

Wire cutters

Round-nose pliers

2—pairs of flat- or chain-nose pliers

Sandpaper

Clear nail polish (optional)

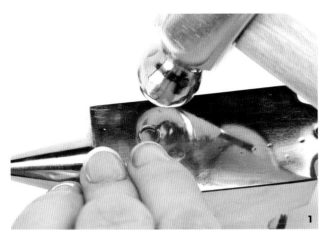

1 Place a copper jump ring in the center of your anvil or steel block. It's round, and your anvil is flat. This is going to be a challenging endeavor, so prepare yourself. Hit the jump ring with the rounded end of the chasing hammer, slowly flattening and texturing the link. The link may fly away. Retrieve it if you can. You can opt to place your finger on one side of the link, but strike carefully to avoid hitting your precious digit!

2 Reconnect the ends of the jump ring if they separate during hammering, making sure to move the ends back together laterally (see page 135 for instructions on opening and closing jump rings). Repeat Steps 1 and 2 for the remaining jump rings.

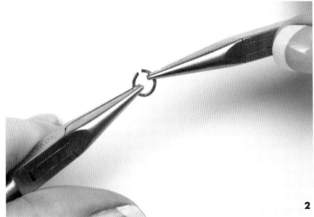

3 Cut four pieces of copper wire to varying lengths. Create a loop in an end of each wire piece using the round-nose pliers (see page 130 for instructions on creating a simple loop).

4 Slowly hammer each wire piece, flattening and texturing the wire as you work from the open end to the bottom of the loop bail.

5 After the wire is sufficiently textured, use your fingers to bend it into squiggly shapes.

6 Sand the end of the wire so it's not too scratchy.

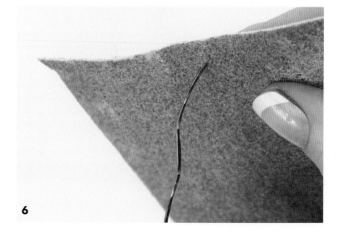

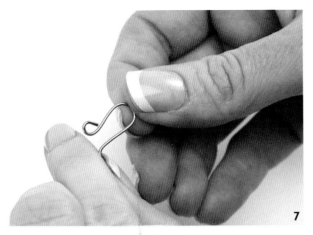

**7**

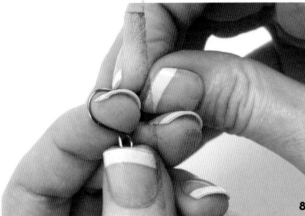

**8**

**9**

7 Cut two 2" (5cm) pieces of wire. Turn a loop in one end of each wire with the round-nose pliers. Bend the center of the wire over your pointer finger and back over itself to make a hook. (Or see page 127 for instructions on creating earring hooks.)

8 Use your fingers to create a slight curve in the hook near the bottom of the wire. Sand the ends of the wire hooks.

9 If you'd like, coat the copper findings with clear nail polish to prevent tarnishing. Create three simple looped beads using the crystals (see page 132 for instructions on creating a simple looped bead). Connect the looped beads with hammered jump rings so that each segment is comprised of three looped beads and three jump rings. Slide the wavy hammered wire segments and the looped bead segments onto a jump ring. Link the earring hook to this component jump ring. Repeat Steps 3 through 9 to make a second earring.

# Peas in a Pod

*By Heidi Boyd, from* Wired Beautiful

There's no question that I often have trouble keeping my peas in a pod. My three children have me running all over the place! This is a case when making jewelry is so much easier than parenting—a little hammering and wrapping is all it takes to keep each set of three beads in place. The pod frame is a snap to make, so you might consider sharing these tidy earrings with friends and family.

## MATERIALS & TOOLS

2—6mm 20-gauge silver-colored-wire jump rings

6—colored stone beads

20-gauge silver-colored wire

24-gauge silver-colored wire

Ring mandrel

Round-nose pliers

Chain-nose pliers

Bent-nose pliers

Wire cutters

Chasing hammer

Steel block

Sanding stick

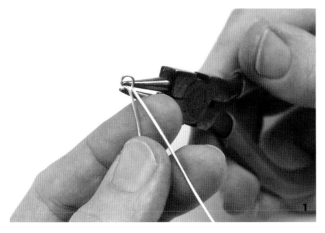

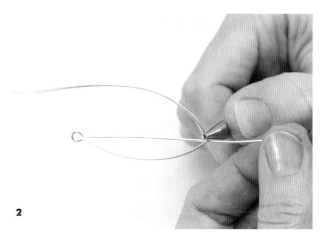

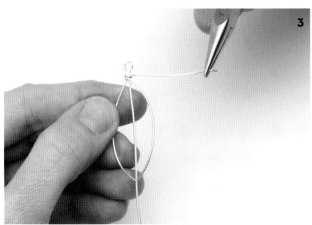

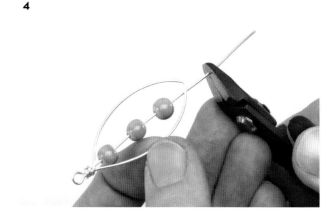

1 Working directly from the spool of 20-gauge wire, create a
  hanging loop by wrapping the wire around the round-nose
  pliers 2¼" (6cm) from the wire end.

2 Use your fingertips to curve the wire (use the wire end
  that is still attached to the spool). Pinch the wire with the
  chain-nose pliers 1½" (4cm) from the base of the loop. Bend
  the wire back up and shape it to make the other half of
  the pod.

3 Using the wire cutters, cut the wire from the spool, leaving
  a 1½" (4cm) tail. Grip the wire tail with the chain-nose pliers
  and wrap the wire around the base of the loop two times.
  Trim the wire end. Use the chain-nose pliers to press the
  cut wire against the base of the loop.

4 String three beads onto the center wire. Trim the wire ¼"
  (6mm) below the base of the pod.

5  Lifting the pod frame out of the way, hammer the $^{3}/_{4}$" (2cm) tip of the center wire on the steel block.

6  Wrap a 4" (10cm) section of 24-gauge wire six times above the $^{3}/_{4}$" (2cm) hammered portion of wire to hold the beads in place. Repeat Steps 1 through 6 to make an identical dangle.

7  Create two earring hooks with the 20-gauge wire (see page 127 for instructions on creating earring hooks). Attach the earring hooks to the loop at the top of each dangle.

5

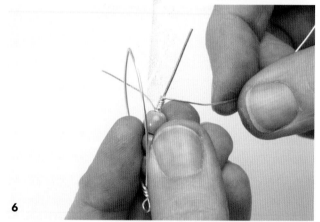

6

7

## Using Files, Sanding Sponges and Sanding Sticks

Filing and sanding wire gives your jewelry a finished look and prevents the wire from catching on clothing and poking the wearer.

After the piece is finished, check it for scratches, pliers indentations and rough edges. Where necessary, apply light pressure and sand the marks smooth. Use the finest files, sanding sticks or sanding sponges last. You should always sand the end of the earring hook that goes through the ear.

You should not sand coated or plated wires because you will remove the finish.

## Polishing Metal

Polishing cloths are the best way to keep your wirework clean and shiny. They quickly wipe away fingerprints and grime. They're essential to have on hand if you're using wire that isn't tarnish-resistant. Always polish your finished piece to make it look its best.

Polishing metal pieces is fast and easy. Using a clean cloth, rub the metal piece until it shines.

## Measuring Wire

Always measure wire before cutting it off the spool. Guessing at measurements will result in different-sized lengths of wire and will cause more work later when the pieces need to be recut or trimmed.

# Snow Queen

*By Julie Ashford, from* Spellbinding Bead Jewelry

These pretty earrings would be fun to wear to a Christmas party or formal dinner and will go with just about any outfit. You can have endless fun experimenting with different bead combinations—maybe introduce a few pearls or some semiprecious chips onto the dangles. The snowflake form is made by twisting wire around cylindrical forms to create stars. Use a wire jig, a ring mandrel or whatever you have that is of a suitable size.

## MATERIALS & TOOLS

28—4mm crystal AB bicone beads

4—6mm crystal AB bicone beads

5 grams—size 10/0 lustre crystal seed beads

1—47" (119cm) length of 20-gauge half-hard silver-plated wire

1—40" (1m) length of 32-gauge soft silver-plated wire

10—2" (5cm) silver-plated headpins

6—2" (5cm) silver-plated eyepins

2—silver-plated earring hooks

Round-nose pliers

Wire cutters

Size 10 beading needle

³/₈" (1cm) cylindrical mold (like a ring mandrel or a dowel)

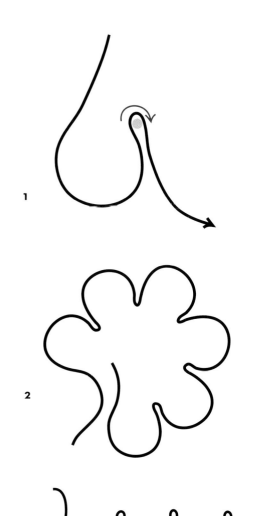

**1**  Measure 4" (10cm) from the end of the 20-gauge wire and wrap the wire three quarters of the way around the $^3/_8$" (1cm) mold. At the end of the curve, grip the wire with the round-nosed pliers and fold it back to touch the wire on the outside of the curve.

**2** Make another five curves and four folds following on from the first to make a rough flower shape. There should not be a fold after final curve.

**3** Gently fold back each adjacent pair of curves so they cross over the tips of each other, forming small loops.

4 Gently open up each curve to bend the wire into a six-pointed star.

5 Complete the last point by wrapping one side of the wire over the other to close up the star shape. Trim the other wire end to ⁵⁄₁₆" (8mm) and roll a loop to match the other points of the star. Trim the wire ends.

6 Fill each point of the star: Cut 40" (1m) of 32-gauge wire and thread it onto the bottom of a point. Thread on: one crystal seed bead, one 4mm bicone and one crystal seed bead. Wrap the wire around the twist at the point of the star. Pass the wire back down the beads, as shown, and move on to the next point. Repeat around the remaining five points. Repeat Steps 1 through 6 to make a second earring.

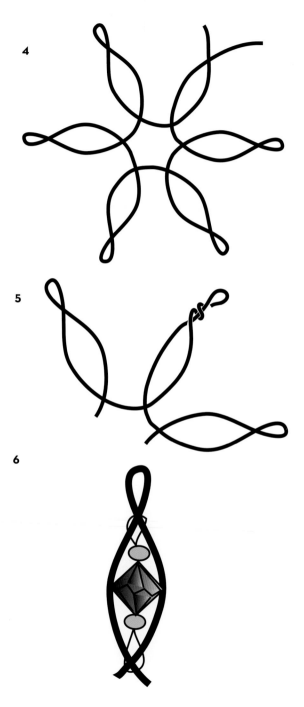

7 For each earring, thread five headpins with one crystal seed bead, one 4mm crystal bicone and one more crystal seed bead. Trim the wires and make a loop at the end of each headpin (see page 130 for instructions on creating a simple loop). Add an eyepin to three of the looped pins, and then add one crystal seed bead, one 4mm crystal bicone, one crystal seed bead to one pin. Add one crystal seed bead, one 6mm crystal bicone and one crystal seed bead to the other two pins. Trim the wires to ¼" (6mm) and make a loop at the end of each eyepin. Link the prepared dangles onto the earring points, as shown at right.

8 Add an eyepin to the top loop and thread on one 4mm crystal bicone. Trim the wire and make a loop. Add an eyepin to that loop and thread on one 6mm crystal bicone. Trim the wire and make a loop as before and then add an earring hook. Repeat Steps 7 and 8 to complete the second earring.

7

# Steel City

*By Margot Potter, from* Bead Chic

Annealed iron wire has a dark and mysterious quality I absolutely love. Faceted freshwater pearls are suspended between the sides of bent and hammered wire. The bright wire is wrapped in a freeform manner for a cocoon-like appearance. Making these wire segments is surprisingly easy and fun. What other designs can you make from this basic idea?

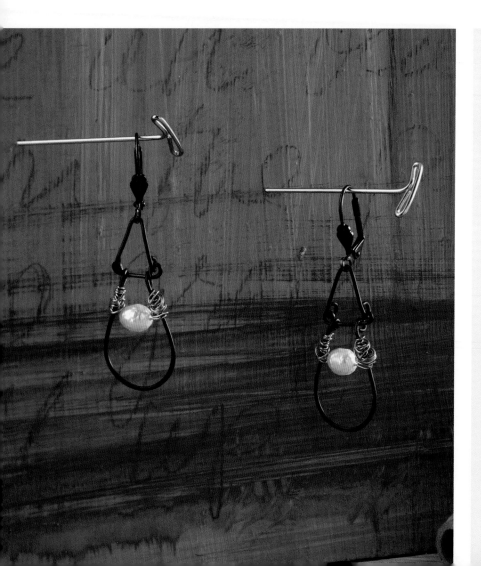

## MATERIALS & TOOLS

2—8mm faceted cream freshwater pearls

24-gauge silver-plated Artistic Wire

20-gauge annealed iron wire

2—gunmetal leverback earring hooks

Chasing hammer

Steel block

Large dowel

Small dowel

Memory wire shears

Round-nose pliers

Chain-nose pliers

Wire cutters

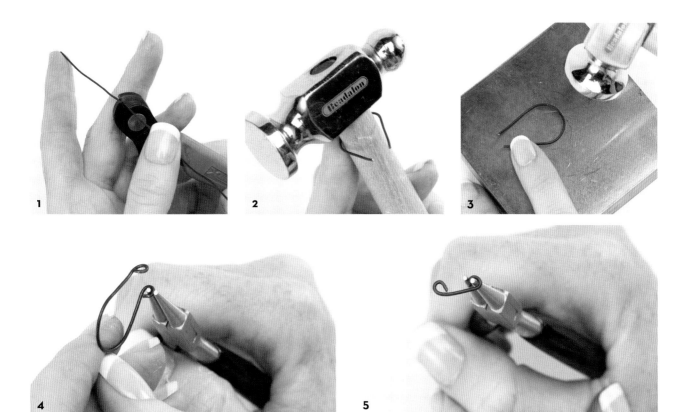

1 Cut a 2½" (6cm) segment of iron wire using the memory wire shears.

2 Bend the center of the wire around the large dowel to create a U shape (I used the handle of my chasing hammer).

3 Hammer the U shape flat using the flat end of the chasing hammer.

4 Create a loop in both wire ends (see page 130 for instructions on creating a simple loop).

5 Cut a ¼" (6mm) section of wire and use the tip of the round-nose pliers to create a very small loop in both ends.

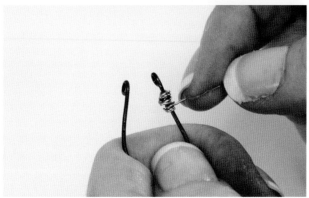

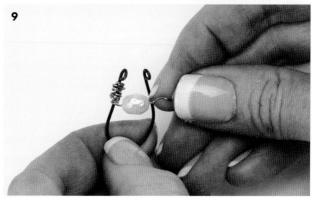

6 Cut a 1¼" (3cm) section of wire and bend it over the the small dowel to form a V shape (I used the metal end of a rattail comb).

7 Use the round-nose pliers to create a loop at both wire ends.

8 Wrap the 24-gauge wire tightly to one side of the top section of the U-shaped component, moving the wire down the core. Continue wrapping the wire around the core in a freeform manner.

9 Thread a pearl onto the 24-gauge wire

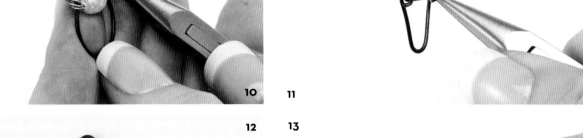

**10**

**11**

**12**

**13**

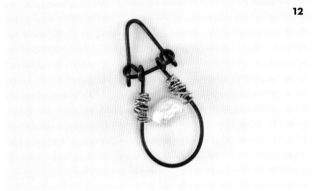

10 Tightly wrap the wire around the opposite side, moving up the core in a freeform manner, as before. Cut off the excess wire with the wire cutters and use the chain-nose pliers to tuck in the wire tails.

11 Connect the segments together as follows: Attach the V-shaped component to the loops on the ends of the bar component.

12 Attach the U-shaped component to the bar. The loops should all face backward so the components can swing freely when worn.

13 Attach an earring hook to the top of each V-section.

# Suspended Coral

*By Heidi Boyd, from* Wired Beautiful

It's incredibly easy to bend wire into a rectangular frame; adding beads to the frame takes just a little wire wrapping. To break the predictability of the frame, irregular, top-drilled coral beads are used here. The juxtaposition makes the finished earrings more interesting. If you have trouble finding the coral beads, a series of round disk beads should have the same contrasting effect.

## MATERIALS & TOOLS

20-gauge half-hard sterling silver wire

24-gauge half-hard sterling silver wire

8–4mm × 10mm red tube coral beads

Ring mandrel

Round-nose pliers

Chain-nose pliers

Bent-nose pliers

Wire cutters

Chasing hammer

Steel block

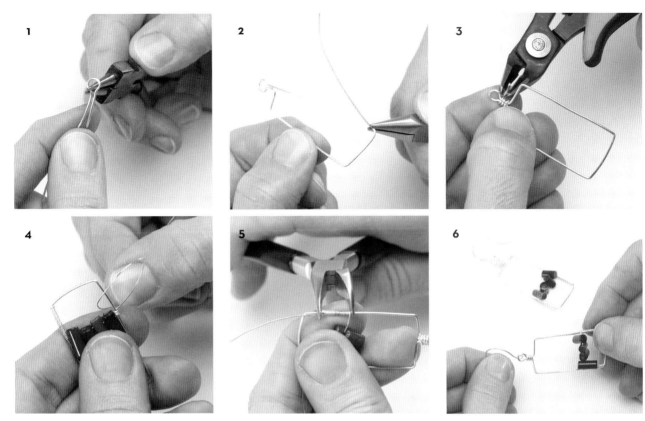

1 Working off a spool of 20-gauge wire, create a hanging loop by wrapping the wire around the round-nose pliers ¼" (6mm) from the wire end. Use the pliers to bend the wire tails out at the base of the loop.

2 After ¼" (6mm) of straight wire, use the chain-nose pliers to bend the wire down to form the top left corner of the rectangle. Bend it again after 1¾" (4cm) to form the bottom left corner, and again after ½" (13mm) to make the bottom right corner. Make a final bend after 1¾" (4cm) to make the top right corner.

3 Using the wire cutters, trim the wire off the spool, leaving a 2" (5cm) tail. Wrap the wire end around the base of the loop ¾" (2cm) from the top right corner. After three wraps, trim both wire ends with the wire cutters.

4 Cut an 8" (20cm) piece of 24-gauge wire. String four coral beads onto the center of the wire. Position the beads across the bottom third of the rectangle. Begin wrapping the wire ends around either side of the rectangle frame.

5 Compress the wrapped wire: Use the bent-nose pliers to squeeze the wrapped wire togther, eliminating any irregular spacing. Continue wrapping down the side until the wraps measure ¾" (2cm). Trim the wires. Repeat Steps 1 through 5 to make a second dangle.

6 Create two earring hooks with the 20-gauge wire (see page 127 for instructions on creating earring hooks). Attach the earring hooks to the hanging loops of the finished dangles.

# Triptych

*By Margot Potter, from* Bead & Wire Jewelry Exposed

I have a three-dimensional brain, and I love working with hard wire because it allows me to create sculptural designs. These earrings are simple wire shapes tightly wrapped with thinner wire. I'm thrilled with how they turned out. Adding the incredibly reflective crystal vitrial rounds gives these funky earrings a touch of sophistication.

## MATERIALS & TOOLS

60 (approximately)—4mm crystal vitrial AB round beads

20-gauge ColourCraft wire in copper, bright blue and mint green

24-gauge silver-plated Colour-Craft wire

Round-nose pliers

Chain-nose pliers

Nylon-jaw pliers

Wire cutters

Bead mat

Safety goggles

Large-grit sandpaper or metal file

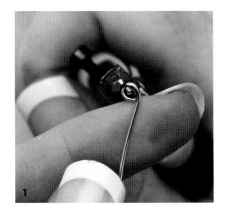
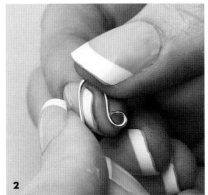
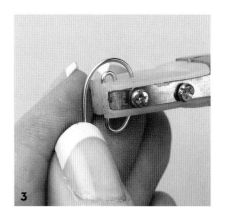

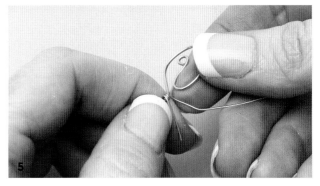

1 Cut two 3" (8cm) sections of 20-gauge wire in each of the following colors: copper, bright blue and mint green. Begin to make the shapes by forming a small loop at the end of one of the bright blue wire pieces with the round-nose pliers (see page 130 for instructions on creating a simple loop).

2 Use your fingers to bend the wire into a U shape in the opposite direction from the loop.

3 Grasp the wire with the nylon-jaw pliers to keep the wire from getting nicked or marred. Loop the wire around to complete the coil. The coil should be about $\frac{1}{2}$" (13mm) in diameter.

4 Trim the wire about $\frac{1}{2}$" (13mm) above the coil, making sure to leave enough excess wire to make a bail. Bend the end of the wire up at a right angle. Grasp the wire at the bend with your round-nose pliers. Bend the wire over the pliers and around to form a rounded bail. Repeat from the end of Step 1 through Step 4 to make another bright blue wire coil, spiraling the wire in the opposite direction to make a mirror image (to create a right and a left earring). Make two copper coils and two mint green coils in the same manner, each in mirrored pairs, and each approximately $\frac{3}{4}$" (2cm) in diameter.

5 Cut a 10" (25cm) section of 24-gauge wire. Beginning at the top of the first wire shape, wrap the wire around the thicker wire four times, leaving a small tail you can grasp while you start the coil.

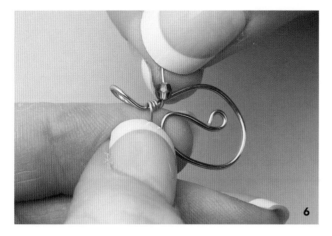

6 String a crystal onto the wire, keeping it flush with the final wire wrap. Bring the wire around the blue wire, securing the crystal in place and keeping the crystal at the front of the shape. Continue wrapping crystals to the wire, approximately 1/8" (3mm) apart, adjusting the wires to keep the crystals to the front and maintaining enough tension that the beads remain in place. Work carefully and wear goggles in case a bead breaks. Continue wrapping your way around the shape until you almost reach the bottom loop. Wrap the thin wire around the core wire tightly four times. Trim away the excess wire and tuck the wire tail under with the chain-nose pliers.

7 Wrap each remaining shape with crystals and secure them with multiple wire wraps, as in Step 6.

8 Attach the sections together by opening and closing the bails around the bottom of each shape. The smaller blue coils should be on top, followed by the larger copper and mint green shapes.

9 Cut two 1 1/2" (4cm) pieces of 20-gauge copper wire. Bend the center of one wire piece over your pointer finger.

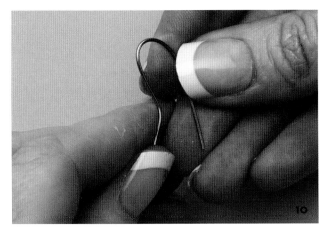

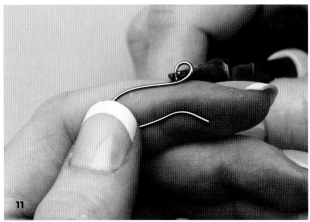

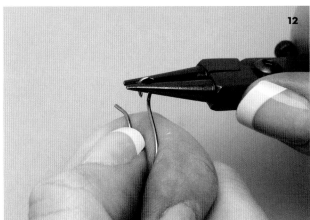

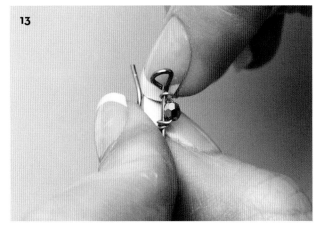

10 Use your fingers or the chain-nose pliers to add a slight bend to one end of the wire.

11 Use the round-nose pliers to make a small loop on the other end of the earring wire.

12 Grasp the loop with the round-nose pliers and bend it up.

13 Wrap a piece of 24-gauge wire around the front of the earring hook twice, and then add a crystal and secure it by wrapping the wire around the core wire two more times. Cut the wire and tuck in the ends. Sand the wire ends lightly to smooth the wires. Link each set of three shapes to the earring hooks.

# Beaded Bead

*by Carole Rodgers, from Beyond Beading Basics*

Vertical netting covers two 20mm round plastic beads to make this pair of earrings. Try plastic beads because they are lightweight—which is important if they'll hang from your ears! Netting can also have a million variables; if you want to cover something other than a 20mm bead, experiment to see how many patterns you'll need and how many beads to put in each pattern. Enjoy!

## MATERIALS & TOOLS

2—black 20mm round plastic beads

6 grams—white size 11/0 pearl seed beads

3 grams—gold-plated size 11/0 seed beads

4—black 6mm bicone crystals

2—2" (5cm) gold headpins

7 links—4mm round link gold chain

2—gold earring hooks

Size 10 or 12 beading needle

1—2 yard (2m) length of 4 lb Fireline or .004" (.13mm) diameter DandyLine, white

Gem-Tac Permanent Adhesive

Round-nose pliers

Wire cutters

Scissors

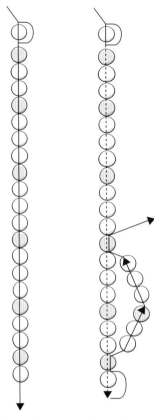

Figure 1.     Figure 2.

## MAKING THE NET

1 Cut 1 yard (1m) of line and single thread your needle.

2 Using a half hitch knot that you can remove later (see below), tie on a white seed bead, leaving an 8" (20cm) tail.

3 Refer to Figure 1 and pick up the following seed beads: one gold (the shared bead), two white (the bridge beads), one gold, three white, one gold, three white, one gold, three white, one gold, two white, one gold and one white to make Row 1.

4 Skip the last white bead and pass the needle back through the last (shared) gold bead, from the bottom up (See Figure 2.)

5 Pick up two white, one gold and three white seed beads, and pass the needle through the third gold bead from the bottom from the underside up. (See to Figure 2.)

# How to Tie a Half Hitch Knot

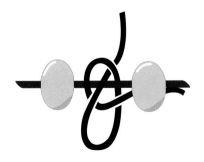

1 Take a small stitch over a thread between two beads in your work and pull the thread through until you have just a small loop of thread left.

2 Pass the needle through the loop (see figure at left) and pull tight.

3 Pass through a few beads and tie another half hitch knot.

4 Apply a very small amount of glue to the thread close to the knot and pass through a few more beads.

5 Pull the thread tight and cut off the excess close to a bead.

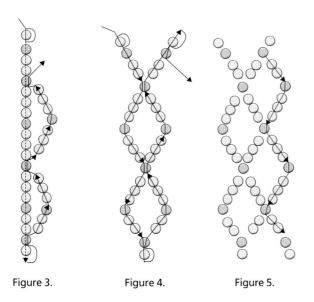

Figure 3.  Figure 4.  Figure 5.

6  Pick up three white, one gold and three white seed beads and pass through the fifth gold bead from the bottom from the underside up, as shown in Figure 3.

7  Pick up two white, one gold and one white seed bead to finish Row 2.

8  Skip the last white bead you picked up and pass the needle through the gold bead just below it to start Row 3, as shown in Figure 4. Continue up and down the piece adding the correct number of seed beads for each section, as shown in Figure 5.

9  Weave nine rows of beading so you have nine points at the top and bottom of the piece.

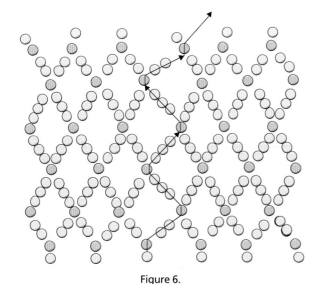

Figure 6.

## JOINING THE NET

1  To join together the ends to form a tube, bring the ends around to meet. Come out of the left bottom point white bead and pass through the next gold bead. (See Figure 6.)

2  String on two white beads and immediately swing over to the next gold bead on the right and pass through it.

3  String on three more white beads and pass through the gold bead on the left.

4  Keep going back and forth across and up the piece, as shown in Figure 6, lacing it together until you get to the original white bead you tied on the end of your thread in the beginning.

5  Leave the knot around the very first bead and tie the two thread ends together to secure.

## COVERING THE 20MM BEAD

1 Using your working thread if you have enough (add a new one if you don't), pass through all the white point beads and gather the threaded beads into a ring.

2 Pass through all the point beads again. Tie a few half hitch knots and work the thread to the other end of the netting, following the pattern (see page 111 for instructions on how to tie a half hitch knots).

3 Place the 20mm bead so the ring of point beads lines up with the hole in the big bead. Run the needle abd thread up through the 20mm bead to the other side.

4 Run the needle through all the point beads on that end and pull tight. Pass the needle through all the point beads a second time

5 Tie half hitch knots and work the tail of the thread into the work. Glue the knot and trim the excess thread.

6 Repeat all steps for the second earring.

## FINISHING THE EARRINGS

1 On one headpin, thread on one gold seed bead, one black crystal, one beaded bead and one black crystal.

2 Trim the pin to ³/₈" (10mm) and turn a loop on the top (see page 130 for instructions on creating a simple loop).

3 Cut the piece of chain in half so you have two pieces, each with three links.

4 Attach a headpin to one end link of a piece of chain.

5 Attach the other end of the chain to the earring hook.

6 Repeat Steps 1 through 5 to make a second earring.

## Tip

*In this project, you create points at the tops and bottoms of the piece. This is how you count the number of rows you need to cover a project. For example, if you need nine rows to go around an item like the bead used in these earrings, you would work the piece until you have nine points on the top and bottom. Keep in mind that the beginning half point and the ending half point are included in that number. When you join the net into a tube, these points will work into the piece.*

# Persephone

*By Julie Ashford, from Spellbinding Bead Jewelry*

These sumptuous earrings remind me of the pomegranate seeds that Persephone ate that bound her to the underworld. Stars and beads are linked together with looped eyepins and jump rings so the earrings flex as you move.

## MATERIALS

2 grams—dark red AB size 10/0 seed beads

2 grams—purple AB size 10/0 seed beads

2—6mm dark red crystal bicone beads

2—4mm orange crystal bicone beads

2—4mm red AB crystal bicone beads

2—4mm dark red crystal bicone beads

1—reel of orange Superlon "AA"

4—very fine ³/₁₆" (5mm) gilt jump rings

2—2" (5cm) gilt headpins

4—2" (5cm) gilt eyepins

2—earring hooks

Scissors

Wire cutters

2—pairs flat- or chain-nose pliers

Round-nose pliers

Size 13 beading needle

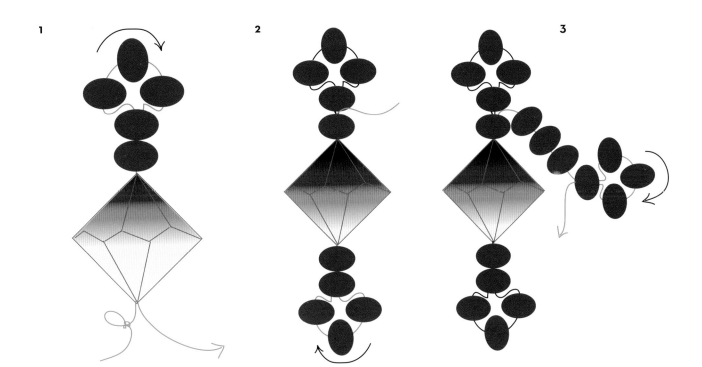

**1** Put aside the four dark red AB size 10/0 seed beads with the largest holes (we'll call these X beads). Prepare the needle with 40" (1m) of single thread and tie a knot 4" (10cm) from the end. Thread on one orange crystal bicone and five dark red AB seeds. Turn the needle and pass it back through the two dark red AB seeds nearest the orange crystal bicone to pull the last three dark red AB seeds into a decorative picot.

**2** Thread on five dark red AB seeds. Turn the needle and pass it back through the two dark red AB seeds nearest the orange crystal bicone, through the bicone and the following one dark red AB seed to make a second picot.

**3** Thread on seven dark red AB seeds. Turn the needle and pass it back through the fourth dark red AB seed just added to bring the last three dark red AB seeds into a picot.

**4**

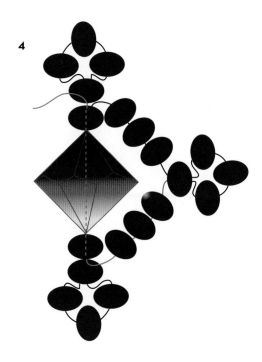

**5**

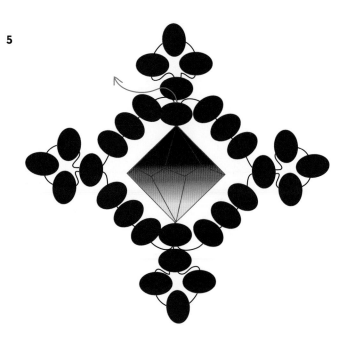

**6**

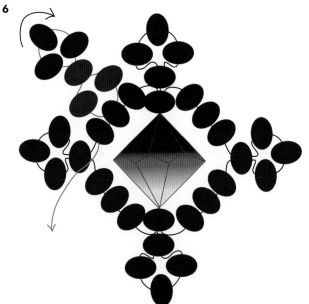

4 Thread on three dark red AB seeds. Pass the needle through the dark red AB seed on the far side of the bicone, the bicone and the following one dark red AB seed.

5 Repeat Steps 3 and 4 to complete the beading around the bicone. Run the needle through the outer beads of the motif to reinforce the shape. Do not tie off the threads at this point.

6 Pass the needle through the first two dark red AB seeds of the strap around the bicone, and thread on two purple AB seeds, one dark red AB seed, one X bead, and one dark red AB seed. Turn the needle and pass it back down the last purple AB seed threaded. Thread on one purple AB seed. Pass the needle through the middle bead of the strap once more and the last purple AB seed of the strap.

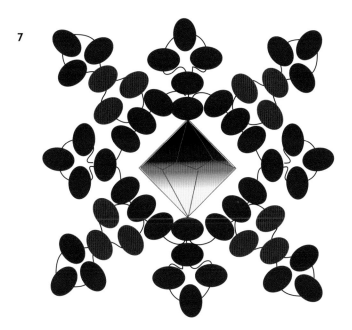

**7** Work the needle through the second dark red AB seed of the next strap around the bicone, and thread on two purple AB seeds and three dark red AB seeds. Turn the needle and pass it back down the last purple AB seed threaded. Thread on one purple AB seed. Pass the needle through the middle bead of the strap once more and the last purple AB seed of the strap. Work the needle around the bicone to the next strap and repeat to make one more spike with an X bead at the end and a final spike in the remaining gap with a dark red AB seed at the end.

**8** Attach a jump ring through each of the X beads at each end of the motif. For the bottom of the earring, thread a headpin with one purple AB seed, one 4mm dark red crystal bicone and one purple AB seed. Trim the wire to $1/4$" (6mm), make a loop and link the headpin onto the bottom jump ring of the star motif (see page 130 for instructions on creating a simple loop).

**9** Attach an eyepin to the top jump ring and thread on one purple AB seed, one 6mm dark red crystal bicone and one purple AB seed. Trim the wire to $1/4$" (6mm) and make a loop. Attach a second eyepin to the loop just made and thread on on one purple AB seed, one 4mm red AB crystal bicone and one purple AB seed. Trim the wire to $1/4$" (6mm) and make a loop, attaching an earring wire to the loop just completed. Repeat Steps 1 through 9 to make a second earring.

# Deco Chic

*By Fernando Dasilva, from* Modern Expressions

The standouts in this project are the modern sterling silver diamond-shaped connectors. When findings are extraordinarily pretty, you don't need to add much to them. Flawless emerald-cut citrine pendants illuminate these earrings, while amethyst pendants and black spinel briolettes add depth to the architectural silhouette.

## MATERIALS

1—24" (61cm) length of 26-gauge sterling silver round half-hard wire

8—8mm × 6mm top-drilled amethyst emerald-cut pendants

4—10mm × 7.5mm top-drilled citrine emerald-cut pendants

2—30mm sterling silver 3-diamond pendants

2—16mm × 14mm × 2mm black spinel fancy-cut triangle briolettes

2—6mm sterling silver jump rings

2—4mm sterling silver jump rings

1—pair of polished modern square ear posts

Wire cutters

Bent chain-nose pliers

Round-nose pliers

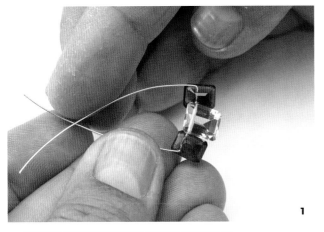

1 String the following beads onto a 4" (10cm) piece of 26-gauge sterling silver wire: one amethyst with the pavilion or back side facing forward, one citrine with the front facing forward and one amethyst with the pavilion side facing forward. Arrange the stones so they sit snugly together in the center of the wire. Bend each side of the wire straight up.

2 Carefully bend the wire on the right side of the component from Step 1 at a right angle approximately ¼" (6mm) above the hole in the amethyst stone. The wire should now be running toward the back of the component. Repeat this step on the left side.

3 Place the component inside the bottom right opening in a diamond pendant. The two wires should be inside the opening. Carefully bend the left-side wire down and over the pendant, then up and around, securing the component. Repeat this step on the right side.

4 Trim the right-side wire, leaving enough excess so it can be pushed through the opening again and bent flat against the diamond pendant (the wire should make 1½ revolutions around the pendant bar). Gently squeeze the end of the wire in the back with the bent chain-nose pliers so the end doesn't stick out. Cut the excess wire. Repeat this on the left side. Repeat Steps 1 through 4 on the opposite side of the diamond pendant.

5 Using a 3" (8cm) piece of sterling wire, string on a spinel drop. Bend both ends of the wire straight up and attach the drop to the bottom of the pendant as instructed in steps 3 and 4. (The wire should make 1½ revolutions around the pendant bar.) Adjust the wraps so the wires form a V shape at the bottom of the pendant and trim any excess wire.

6 Attach a 6mm jump ring to the top V shape of the diamond pendant. Attach a 4mm jump ring to the 6mm jump ring. Attach an earring post to the 4mm jump ring. Repeat Steps 1 through 6 for the other earring.

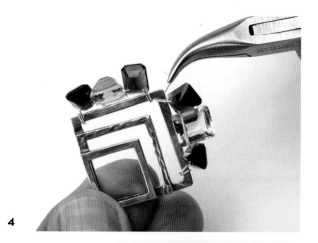

4

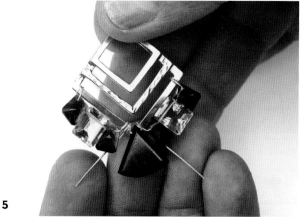

5

6

# Fernando Dasilva's Best Tips and Tricks

*(From* Modern Expressions)

"In my mind, jewelry and clothing are the only true artistic expressions for transforming ideas into body adornments. Rocks, paper, plastic, crystals, gemstones, feathers, glass, natural fibers, seeds, terra-cotta, leather, leaves, metal, wood—all of these elements can be transformed into visual artistic expressions."

~Fernando

## Tip

*A printed boho silk blouse is a fabulous choice to accentuate the retro cool style of these chandelier earrings. Big earrings are helpful in drawing the eye away from an ample bust.*

Illustration by Vladimir Alvarez

# Japanese Diamonds

*by Rebeca Mojica, from Chained*

The pattern is basic, but working with tiny rings is tricky! With 50 jump rings per earring, this project takes a bit of time. The end result is well worth it, however—a svelte pair of earrings that can be color-customized to match your favorite outfit.

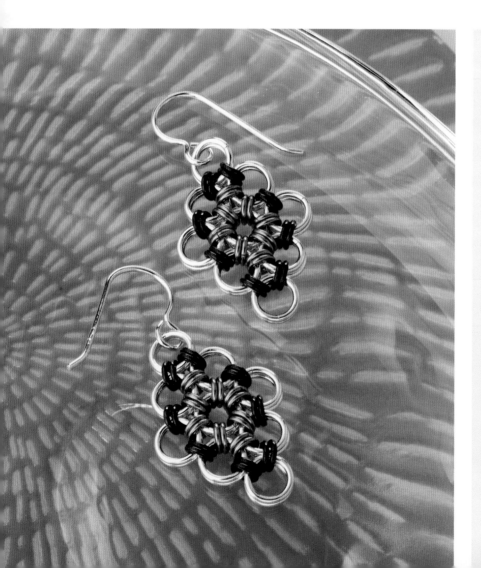

## MATERIALS

36—medium jump rings: G19 sterling, 19 gauge, $^{11}/_{64}$" (4.4mm)

64—tiny jump rings: B20 anodized niobium, 20 gauge, $^{3}/_{32}$" (2.4mm):

> 32—brown
>
> 32—green

2—earring hooks

2—pairs of flat-nose pliers with narrow jaws or 2 pairs of chain-nose pliers

**1**
**2**
**3**

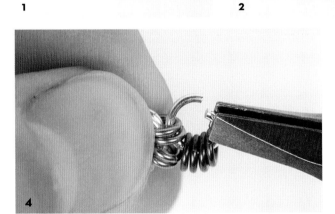

**4**
**5**

1 To prepare, open the medium rings (see page 135 for instructions on opening and closing jump rings). Close sixteen of the brown rings, and open the other sixteen. Close twenty-four of the green rings, and open the remaining eight. Pick up eight tiny green rings with a medium ring and then close the medium ring.

2 Double the medium ring with a new medium ring. Add another open tiny green ring to the large rings and close.

3 To finish the center of the pattern, add three more open tiny green rings to the doubled medium rings, closing each after it is added. (The reason you don't begin with all 12 green rings on the medium ring in Step 1 is that with all those small rings you wouldn't have enough room to get your pliers in there to close the medium ring!)

4 Scoop four closed brown rings onto a medium ring and go through two of the hanging green rings. Close this medium ring and then double it with another medium ring. When adding the second ring, it is usually easier to come up through the green rings first, and as you continue moving the ring, use the fingers of your nondominant hand to slide the brown rings onto the open medium ring. When you're through all six rings, close the second medium ring.

5 You will now start working your way around the center, going through two pairs of adjacent hanging tiny rings—one pair from the previous set of medium rings and one pair from the center. With a new medium ring, scoop up two green rings. Weave the medium ring through two brown rings and two green rings. Close the medium ring and double it.

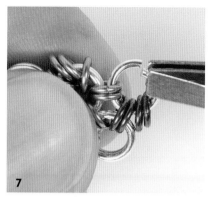
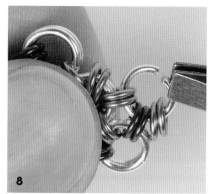

6 Next, scoop two brown rings onto a new medium ring and go through the two green hanging rings from the previous medium ring and two green rings from the center. Close the medium ring and double it.

7 Scoop two more brown rings onto a new medium ring and go through the two brown rings on the previous medium ring and the next two green rings in the center. Close the medium ring and double it.

8 Continue around the center ring: Scoop two green rings onto a new medium ring and go through the two brown rings on the previous medium ring and the next two green rings in the center. Close this medium ring and then double it.

9 With a new medium ring, go through the remaining six hanging rings—two green rings from the previous medium ring, two green rings from the center and the two free brown rings on the first medium ring from Step 4. Do not add any more tiny rings to this medium ring.

10 Double the ring from Step 9. Be careful not to open it too wide, or you'll have difficulty closing the ring. To help close the ring, you can sandwich it between your pliers as shown, and then fine-tune the closure as you normally would with two pliers. (Before sandwiching, be sure to first spin the first ring around so the closure is hidden on the inside of the weave.)

**11**

11 Add two open brown rings to each set of medium rings that is currently only connected to two brown rings. The brown rings now form a diamond outline.

12 Go through four adjacent hanging brown rings with a new medium ring and close it. Double that ring.

13 Repeat Step 12 on the other side of the weave, but add the earring hook before closing the medium rings. Repeat all steps to make a second earring.

## *Variation:*

*Try this weave pattern in your favorite colors, or for an even more elegant pair of earrings, enhance the pattern with beads and additional rings. The pair on the left uses 4mm beads and bicone crystals, and (lots) more B20 sterling and niobium rings.*

# *5*

# *Techniques for Making Earrings*

Nothing is more important to the success and joy of your jewelry-making endeavors than developing good technique. It's the key to making it fun and easy and, more important, to producing jewelry pieces that look professional. This chapter begins with instructions for creating for a variety of earring hook styles and then moves into the simple, everyday techniques you'll use throughout the projects.

Although earring hooks can be easily purchased at any craft or jewelry supply store, handmade hooks can really set a pair of earrings apart from standard store-bought earrings. Artistic hooks are surprisingly simple, fun and inexpensive to make. When deciding on earring hooks, consider the shapes of the beads you are working with.

Sterling silver or gold-filled wire, 20- or 21-gauge, are good choices for making earring hooks. There are a few tools that will be helpful when making earring hooks—see the earring hook tool kit, on pages 12 and 13. A variety of earring hook shapes and sizes are shown here, but with a little practice, you'll be adapting them to meet your needs in no time at all!

## *Tip*

*Don't forget: No matter what type of earring hooks you make, sand the cut wire ends to make them more comfortable when passing through the earlobe. See page 95 for more information on using files, sanding sponges and sanding sticks.*

# CREATING EARRING HOOKS: SIMPLE FRENCH HOOKS

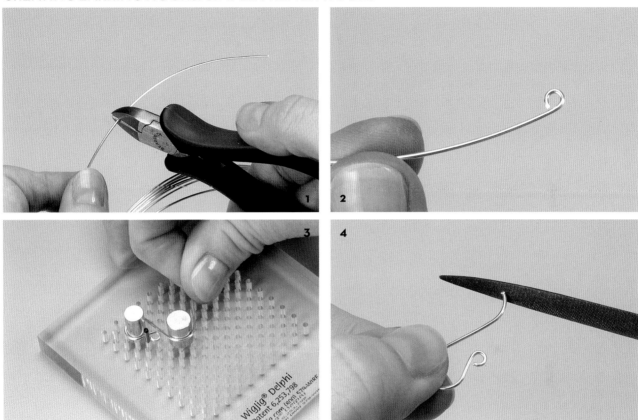

1 Cut 2¼"–3½" (6cm–9cm) of wire, depending on the curve radius and the length of the tail that you desire.

2 Grab the end of the wire with round-nose pliers and wrap one full turn of the wrist, making a P shape.

3 In the opposite direction of this small loop, press the wire against the barrel of a smooth pen or use a wire jig. (See page 13 for a sample wire-jig layout.) When using a pen, slightly bend up the last ¼" (6mm) of the tail with the chain-nose pliers, if desired.

4 File in one direction with a needle file to smooth any rough edges. If desired, flatten the tail of the hook with a chasing hammer (see page 135 for more information about hammering). If you prefer the rounded shape of the wire, use the hard plastic mallet to work-harden the wire (see page 135 for more information on work-hardening).

## CREATING EARRING HOOKS: SIMPLE WIRE HOOPS

In this earring style, part of the wire of the hoop goes directly through the ear. Therefore, when adding beads, it's important to leave at least ½" (13mm) at the front of the earring to accommodate the thickness of the earlobe. General sizes of wire: for 1" (3cm) hoops, use 4" (10cm) of wire; for 1¼" (3cm) hoops, use 5" (13cm) of wire; for 1½" (4cm) hoops, use 5½" (14cm) of wire. Using half-hard sterling silver or gold-filled wire will ensure the hoops retain their shape.

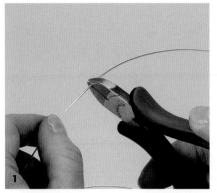
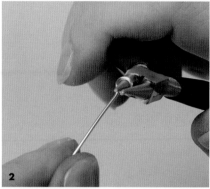

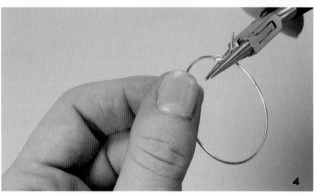
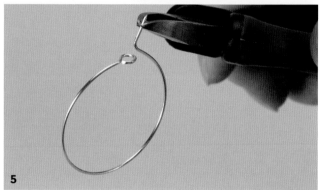

1 Before cutting the 20- or 21-gauge wire, run nylon-jaw pliers over it a few times to straighten it. Cut two pieces of the wire, using the suggestions above to determine the length.

2 At the end of the wire, create a simple or wire-wrapped loop (see pages 130 and 131 for instructions on creating simple and wire-wrapped loops).

3 Wrap the wire around the base of a ring mandrel or a 1" (3cm) object—or to desired size. The wire will spring into a circle when released. If you plan to thread beads on the hoop, do so now.

4 At the point where the end of the wire crosses past the loop, use round-nose pliers to bend the wire up 90 degrees to create a smooth curved bend.

5 Cut the tail about ¼" (6mm) long. File it smooth.

# CREATING EARRING HOOKS: ROUND EARRING HOOKS

These big, round earring hooks have a modern, bold style that is decidedly artistic. They're perfect to pair with round focal beads.

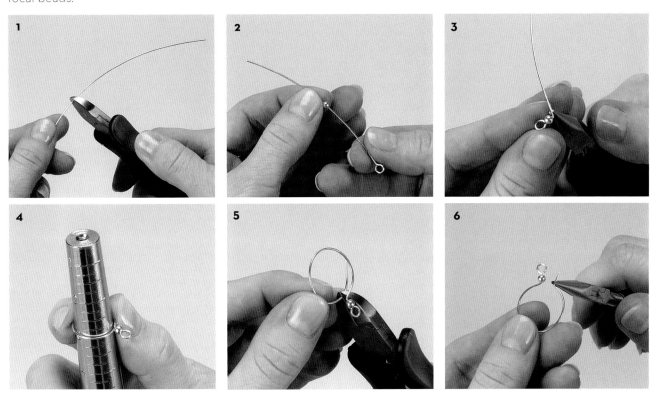

1 Cut two pieces of 20- or 21-gauge wire each about 3"–3½" (8cm–9cm) long, depending on the desired diameter. (If needed, straighten the wire before cutting.)

2 At the end of the wire, create a simple loop (see page 130 for instructions on creating a simple loop). If desired, you can add a 2mm or 3mm spacer, crystal or other small bead at the base to decorate the hook.

3 Using chain-nose pliers, bend the wire 90 degrees toward the front of the hook, taking care not to crush the accent bead, if applicable.

4 Grasp the loop end with your forefinger and thumb and press it firmly around the mandrel. Wrap the wire all the way around the mandrel until it reaches past the loop. Release the wire.

5 Use wire cutters to snip any excess wire that reaches past the loop.

6 Bend the last ¼" (6mm) of the wire end back slightly and file to smooth any sharp ends.

## CREATING A SIMPLE LOOP

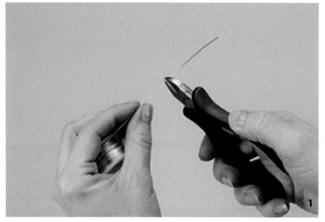

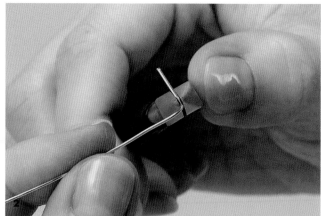

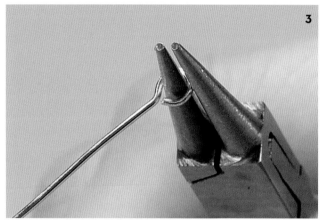

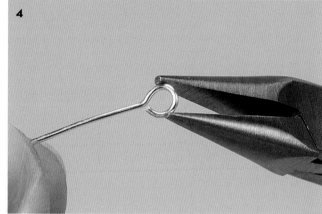

1 Using wire cutters, cut about 2" (5cm) of 24- or 26-gauge wire.

2 About ³⁄₈" (1cm) from the end of the wire, bend the wire 90 degrees with chain-nose pliers.

3 With round-nose pliers, grab the short end of the wire. Turn your wrist toward your body and release the wire. Repeat until the end of the wire meets the base, forming a complete circle.

4 If necessary, carefully close any gaps using chain-nose pliers. Apply gentle pressure to avoid crushing the loop.

# CREATING A WIRE-WRAPPED LOOP

As your skills grow, I recommend using a wire-wrapped loop whenever possible in your designs. It provides a professional and polished look, and your jewelry will be far more durable. This loop is more time-consuming and can't be reopened. However, because there are no open loops, there are fewer opportunities for pieces to come loose.

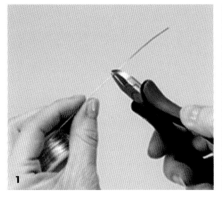

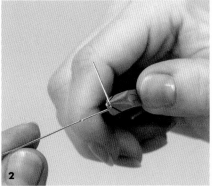

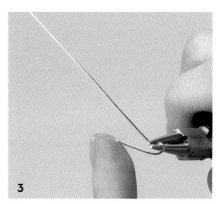

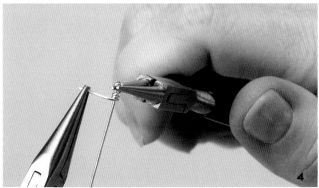

1 Using wire cutters, cut about 2"–2½" (5cm–6cm) of 24- or 26-gauge plated or copper practice wire.

2 About 1" (3cm) from the end of the wire, bend the wire 90 degrees with chain-nose pliers.

3 Position round-nose pliers so they sit directly in the corner of the angle you made in Step 2. With your fingers, press

the tail of the wire around the round jaw of the round-nose pliers one time.

4 Grab the short end of the wire with chain-nose pliers and wrap it around the base of the loop two or three times to secure it. Release the wire and reposition your wrist and the chain-nose pliers as needed.

5 Cut off the excess wire with wire cutters.

## CREATING A SIMPLE LOOPED BEAD

Making beaded jewelry is simple—it's just a matter of completing one step, then adding the next! To make a looped bead, start by Creating a Simple Loop (see page 130), then start here with Step 1.

1  Complete Steps 1 through 4 for Creating a Simple Loop (see page 130), and slide a bead onto the end of the remaining wire.

2  Bend the remaining wire 90 degrees with the chain-nose pliers in the same direction as the loop below the bead. Cut the end to about ³⁄₈" (1cm) long. Or, to make a wire-wrapped looped bead, don't cut the wire until you've wrapped it around the loop two to three times.

3  With the round-nose pliers, grab the short end of the wire. Turn your wrist toward your body and release the wire. Grab the wire again and turn your wrist until the end of the wire matches up with the base in a complete circle.

4  If necessary, carefully close any gaps with the chain-nose pliers. Apply gentle pressure to avoid crushing the loop.

# CREATING A LOOPED DANGLE

With the basic technique you learned in Creating a Simple Loop (see page 130), you can create dangles for your earrings. And while we won't show instructions here, it will be very easy, using the Creating a Wire-Wrapped Loop instructions (see page 131), to adapt these instructions to create a wire-wrapped loop dangle.

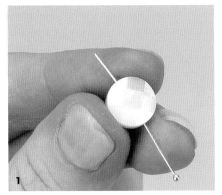 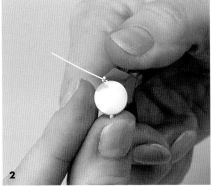 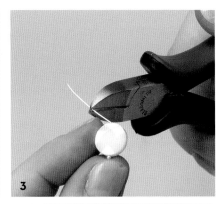

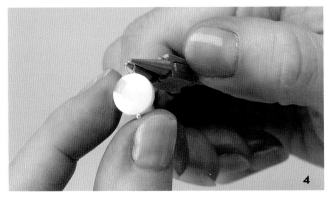 

1 Slide the bead or beads onto a headpin.

2 With chain-nose pliers, bend the headpin wire to 90 degrees directly above the top of the bead.

3 Cut the end of the wire to about ³⁄₈" (1cm) in length.

4 Hold the bead in your hand and grab the short end of the wire with round-nose pliers. Begin to turn your wrist to form a loop. Release the wire and reposition your wrist and the round-nose pliers as needed.

5 With the chain-nose pliers, carefully close up any gaps in the loop. Apply gentle pressure to avoid crushing the loop.

## WRAPPING WIRE AROUND A BASE

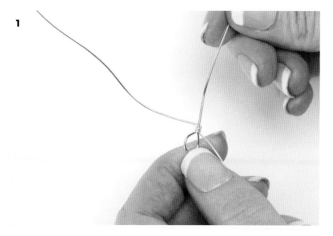

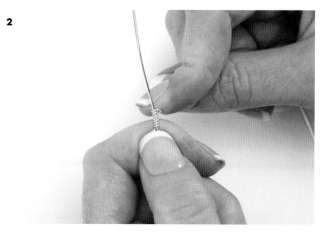

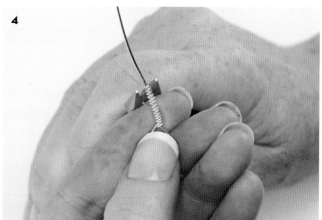

1 Wire wrapping around a base can be done with a wire already attached to the base, or with a wire you add. The wire you wrap around the base is called the "working wire." Wrap the working wire tightly around the end of the base or core wire.

2 Continue wrapping with tension, working up the core wire and using your pointer finger to keep the wire flush as you work.

3 When you reach the desired length, cut off the excess wire with the wire cutters.

4 Use chain-nose pliers to tuck the wire tail under.

## OPENING AND CLOSING JUMP RINGS

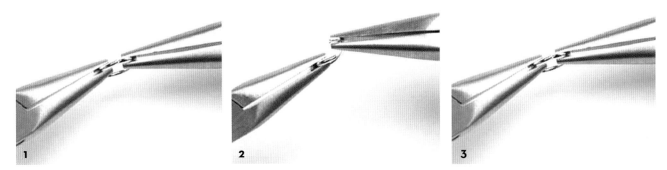

1 Using two pairs of flat- or chain-nose pliers, grasp the jump ring on either side of the break in the tips of the jaws of the pliers. (If you don't have two pairs of flat- or chain-nose pliers, you can use a pair of bent-nose pliers in place of one of the pairs.)

2 The key to opening a jump ring is to move the pliers in opposition to each other instead of out from the center. If you open a jump ring by pulling the ends apart, the metal becomes stressed and the circle loses its shape. Open the ring laterally so one end is moving toward you and one end is moving away from you.

3 When you are ready to close the jump ring, grasp the ends in your pliers and move them past each other, as you did before, gently compressing them together as you move them. Move the ends past each other again, but this time you should feel them click into place. This means you've created tension and the jump ring should remain closed. If they don't click, keep passing them while gently compressing them until they are secure.

## HAMMERING

1 Place your wire or metal component flat on your steel block on a sturdy, solid work surface. While holding onto your wire or metal components, carefully but firmly strike the object using the appropriate hammer for the effect you desire. If your piece bends up due to the hammering, hammer it flat with a hard plastic mallet. This mallet will work-harden and flatten the piece without removing the hammered effect.

### *Tip*

*Work-hardening is the stiffening that occurs when you bend or work with your wire. You'll want to work-harden some of your metalwork so your handmade earring hooks and other hoops retain their shape.*

# About the Authors

## JULIE ASHFORD

Julie Ashford began designing and making jewelry as a teenager and opened her first shop, Spellbound, in her hometown of Birmingham when she was just 19 years old.

The interest from others wishing to learn beading was so great that Julie taught workshops and started to design kits. In 1994 the business settled in Lichfield, Staffordshire, where thousands of beads are on display and where more than 300 of Julie's kits are available. Julie teaches a range of classes, specializing in wire-based jewelry-making classes. Julie also teaches throughout the U.K. and frequently travels to Japan for teaching engagements. Spellbound celebrated 25 years in business in 2009.

Julie is co-author of *Spellbinding Bead Jewelry*, and author of *Spellbound Festive Beading* and *Starting to Make Bead Jewelry*.

To learn more about Julie and Spellbound, visit www.spellboundbead.co.uk.

## HEIDI BOYD

Heidi Boyd is the author of thirteen craft books with North Light Books, most notably the *Simply Beautiful* series. Her goal is to make sophisticated design approachable and easy for all. She has a fine arts degree and got her start in professional crafting as a contributor to *Better Homes and Gardens* books and magazines. She contributes to national craft publications and loves teaching craft workshops to children and adults.

Heidi, her husband, Jon, and their three children enjoy the natural beauty of their midcoast Maine home.

Stop by her blog, www.heidiboyd.blogspot.com, for more project ideas.

## FERNANDO DASILVA

Fernando Dasilva is a jewelry designer, published author, instructor, blogger and avid chef. His work is as versatile as his personality, from demure sophistication to over-the-top extravaganza.

*Women's Wear Daily* highlighted Fernando as "a designer to watch." He contributes to several beading magazines and jewelry design inspiration books, and he is the only male Create Your Style with Swarovski Elements ambassador. He creates one-of-a-kind jewelry pieces for Beadalon and John Bead Corp. and has designed for Touchstone Crystal and Made By Me Jewelry.

Fernando's first solo book, *Modern Expressions*, was "highly recommended" by *Harper's Bazaar* as a must-read book in the do-it-yourself segment. His jewelry collection is sold through www.dasilvajewelry.com and he writes about jewelry on his blog, www.modern-expressions.blogspot.com.

## SHARILYN MILLER

Sharilyn Miller is a jewelry artist, designer and author with more than a decade of experience teaching various arts and crafts to adult students throughout the United States and overseas. She has written nine popular arts-and-crafts books, including *Rubber Stamped Jewelry*, *Contemporary Copper Jewelry* and *Wire Art Jewelry Workshop*. She is perhaps best known for *Bead on a Wire*, a bestselling wire-art jewelry book published by F+W Media.

Offering "Wild Wire Women" jewelry retreats in her mountain home in Idyllwild, California, Sharilyn also enjoys taking groups of artists to Mexico and Europe for unique art-related adventures. For more information about her workshop retreats and to see her current teaching schedule, visit www.SharilynMiller.com.

Sharilyn also has produced a series of instructional DVDs on wire jewelry making. To learn more, visit www.WireJewelryDVDs.com.

# About the Authors

## REBECA MOJICA

Rebeca Mojica is an award-winning chainmaille artist and instructor and author of the book *Chained*. By using colorful rings and combining classic weaves in new ways, she has redefined this ancient craft. At current count, this self-taught artist knows more than one hundred weaves, including more than a dozen patterns of her own creation.

Rebeca has been teaching maille for almost as long as she has been making it. She helps students discover that they too can create beauty using only their hands, pliers and jump rings.

When she had difficulty finding high-quality supplies for her designs, Rebeca founded Blue Buddha Boutique, with a focus on manufacturing and selling precision-sized and polished rings. The company is now one of the largest chainmaille suppliers in the world.

Visit www.bluebuddhaboutique.com for more information.

## MARGOT POTTER

Margot Potter is a woman of diverse talents and interests. A long time F+W author, she has written seven humorous how-to jewelry-making titles and contributed to countless others. She recently signed on as the resident jewelry-making guru at Jewelry Television for their budding Jewel School program where she appears on live TV, creates content for the web and is creating a series of DVDs. Margot has consulted with and designed for most of the biggest names in the jewelry-making and craft industries including Swarovski, Beadalon, JoAnn Fabrics, AC Moore, I Love to Create and many more. Margot's no-nonsense approach to creative expression demystifies the creative process for the Average Joe and Jane, inviting everyone to the creative table and convincing all of them that they too can "Create Without Filters."

Visit Margot's website, www.margotpotter.com, for more information.

## CAROLE RODGERS

Carole Rodgers is an internationally known designer, author and teacher. She has been a professional designer for the past 26 years and had an extensive career in art education and art therapy prior to that. Carole is the sole author of 99 needlework, crafting and beading-pattern leaflets, hundreds of magazine articles, and three full-length beading books: *Beaded Jewelry with Found Objects*, *Beading Basics* and *Beyond Beading Basics*. She has also been included in numerous compilation books. She sells her line of self-published beading books and kits at retail shows.

Carole and her husband, LeRoy, also sell beads, gemstone cabochons and jewelry-making supplies at retail bead and jewelry shows while they travel the country in their RV. The couple have two daughters and two grandchildren.

## SARA SCHWITTEK

An obsession for color, texture and diverse materials is what keeps Sara Schwittek passionately creating her modern and vintage-inspired designs for Shy Siren, her line of handcrafted jewelry. Formally trained as an architect, Sara taps into her design skills to make new creations of a different scale. Sara has also worked in the architecture design industry and in web design. She and her husband, Michael, currently run www.FourEyes.com, a web design studio.

Sara's diverse background in all things design gives her a unique perspective; she creates each design with an eye toward aesthetics and functionality, finding delight in the craftsmanship and details and in the play of light and color of the materials she works with.

Sara also enjoys photography, yoga and traveling for a good meal. You can see more of her work at www.ShySiren.com. She is the author of *Perfect Match: Earring Designs for Every Occasion*.

# This Book Features Projects From These Great F+W Media, Inc. Titles:

**Bead & Wire Jewelry Exposed**
*by Margot Potter, Fernando Dasilva and Katie Hacker*

**Bead Chic** *by Margot Potter*

**Bead on a Wire** *by Sharilyn Miller*

**Beading Basics** *by Carole Rodgers*

**Beyond Beading Basics** *by Carole Rodgers*

**Beyond the Bead** *by Margot Potter*

**Chained** *by Rebeca Mojica*

**The Impatient Beader Gets Inspired!**
*by Margot Potter*

**Modern Expressions** *by Fernando Dasilva*

**Perfect Match** *by Sara Schwittek*

**Simply Beaded Bliss** *by Heidi Boyd*

**Simply Beautiful Beaded Jewelry** *by Heidi Boyd*

**Spellbinding Bead Jewelry** *by Julie and Christine Ashford*

**Wired Beautiful** *by Heidi Boyd*

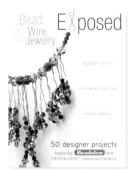

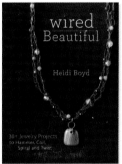

# Index

www.fwmedia.com

15   14   13        5   4   3   2

Distributed in Canada by Fraser Direct
100 Armstrong Avenue
Georgetown, ON, Canada  L7G 5S4
Tel: (905) 877-4411

Distributed in the U.K. and Europe by F&W MEDIA INTERNATIONAL
Brunel House, Newton Abbot, Devon, TQ12 4PU, England
Tel: (+44) 1626 323200, Fax: (+44) 1626 323319
Email: enquiries@fwmedia.com

Distributed in Australia by Capricorn Link
P.O. Box 704, S. Windsor NSW, 2756 Australia
Tel: (02) 4577-3555

ISBN 978-1-4403-1424-7
SRN W1594

Edited by Kristy Conlin
Designed by Corrie Schaffeld
Production coordinated by Greg Nock
Photography by Ric Deliantoni, Christine Polomsky, Hal Barkan, Tim Grodin, Kim Sayer,
    Sylvia Bissonette, Jenna L. Deidel, John Carrico (Alias Imaging, LLC) and Adam Henry (Alias Imaging, LLC)
Styled by Lauren Emmerling, Nora Martini, Jan Nickum, Monica Skrzelowski and Cass Smith
Illustration on page 121 by Vladimir Alvarez

## Metric Conversion Chart

| To convert | to | multiply by |
| --- | --- | --- |
| Inches | Centimeters | 2.54 |
| Centimeters | Inches | 0.4 |
| Feet | Centimeters | 30.5 |
| Centimeters | Feet | 0.03 |
| Yards | Meters | 0.9 |
| Meters | Yards | 1.1 |

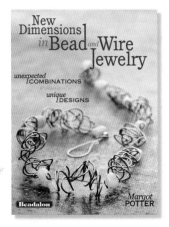